MONDAY MORNING COFFEE

MONDAY MORNING COFFEE

52 Weekly Cups Of Encouragement

by
Cynthia A. Bradley

copyright 2012
Mayfair Press

MONDAY MORNING COFFEE
by Cynthia A. Bradley
Published by Mayfair Press
Huntsville, AL
©2011 all rights reserved

No part of this book may be reproduced
or used in any form without
written permission of the publisher
except for brief excerpts for review purposes

Scripture quotations are taken from the Holy Bible
New International Version Copyright 1973, 1978, 1984
by International Bible Society
Used by permission of Zondervan
and
The Message, by Eugene Peterson
Copyright 1993, 1996, 2000, 2002
Used by permission of NavPress Publishing Group

Printed in the United States of America
Second Edition 2012

ISBN # 978-1-4675-0107-1

Printed by
Colorwise Printing, Inc.
Roswell, GA

designed & edited by Lee Milam

the author can be reached at:
cindi@mayfairpress.org

to order additional copies, go to:
www.mayfairpress.org

Dear Heavenly Father,
It is with a grateful and humble heart that I present this book.
I am thankful for the one who has chosen to read my writings
and allow me to open my heart to them.
May lives be blessed and hearts be touched,
but, first and foremost, may this reader draw closer to You
and to Your son, Jesus.
May all of the praise be given to You alone
as You reign in my life forever.

To my Grandmother, Otis Bradley
Whom we affectionately called "Wo"
No book could hold all the lessons you taught me
I miss you every day
(and I still love it when I'm called "Little Otis")

Acknowledgements

Wayne Kilpatrick - You will always be **my** preacher. Thank you for telling me to write this book.

Stuart and Brenda Mitchell - Your support and encouragement are immeasurable.

My Bonco Sisters - Ann Minor, Jo Gray, Linda Tallon, Linda King, Phyllis Watson, Jane Smith, Loweeda Mitchell, Donna Pate, Martha Kimbrough, Pat Roberson and Martha Stewart. What amazing friends you are. Every second Tuesday of the month is filled with laughter, good food and share time. Thanks for including me.

Renee Graham - You are my rock!

My church families in other cities where I've lived - Landmark in Montgomery; Homewood in Birmingham and East Brainerd in Chattanooga.

The great Mayfair Church of Christ - You've never treated me like a "PK" but, rather a daughter and sister.

My dear friends from my years at Lipscomb University - In four short years you gave me a lifetime of friendships. Thank you Nancy Morrison, Lynn Henderson, Phyllis and P.R. Anderson, Vickie Weatherly, Jennifer Whitehorn, Joy Brown and all of my Pi Delta sisters.

My fellow Beach Bums - Mary Milam, Laura Pendergrass and Regina Cook. I can't wait to be in the southeast corner of heaven with all of you because you know there's a beautiful beach up there.

My friends at Huntsville Hospital - you've all taught me, trained me, amazed me and supported me. The lives you save and touch are immeasurable. May God always honor your efforts.

Kelley and Judy Riley - You were my Alabama family in Tennessee and I cherish you and your family very much.

Karen Brunner - I value your friendship. Being your maid of honor was truly one of the highest honors of my life.

Jill and Bill Speight - Both of you are my counselors, advisors and true friends.

Tripp, Will, Clay, Ben, Autrey, Lucy, Mackenzie and Paisley - I love you all as my very own. I'm honored to be your Aunt Cindi.

My brother, Gary - You've seen midnight so many times but some how you've always fought to see the "joy in the morning". Psalm 30:5.

My brother, Philip - My teacher, my protector, my comedian, my best friend. I love you.

Sisty Bates - You're the sister I never had and I love you dearly. Sometimes I don't know where my family ends and yours begins.

Melisa Blanton - You're the baby sister I never had. My forever friend whom I love dearly.

Thanks to our proof readers - Sue Bell, Wendy Cantrell, Tina Crews, Karen Milam, Tamra Reynolds, Renee Graham.

My heart is overwhelmed with gratitude to Mike and Christine Wicks. Your generosity, support and belief in me and this project is humbling and very much appreciated.

Lee Milam - You saw potential in me and made this happen. Without you, there is absolutely no way this book would have become a reality.

Finally, to my Parents, Gary & Bobbie Bradley - this book is composed of many words but somehow I could never come up with any to tell you both how much I love you and how truly thankful I am to be your daughter.

Contents

JANUARY

1. Are You Warm Enough? - p.2
2. I'm Right Here - p.4
3. Wo - p.6
4. Be Found In Him - p.10
5. Rescue The Perishing - p.12

FEBRUARY

1. We All Need Open Heart Surgery - p.14
2. What's In Your Heart? - p.16
3. Bridge Builders - p.18
4. Where Y'all From? - p.20

MARCH

1. A Nurse Wears Many Hats - p.22
2. A Lesson From Jimmy Buffett? - p.26
3. Cutting Down The Nets - p.28
4. Martha, Martha - p.30
5. I Want To See Jesus - p.32

APRIL

1. But, I'm A Doctor - p.34
2. He Picks Me Every Time - p.36
3. First You've Got To Die - p.38
4. After The Storm - p.40

MAY

1. Stain That Reminds Me of Pain - p.42
2. I Want My Mommy - p.44
3. I've Got The Power - p.46
4. Anger- Is It Worth It? - p.48
5. Catch Me, Daddy - p.50

JUNE

1. The Mask Will Appear - p.52
2. Hand Over The Wheel - p.54
3. I Need To Call My Dad - p.56
4. Parenting Is Not For Wimps - p.58

JULY

1. Call The Lifeguard - p.60
2. What's Your Thorn? - p.62
3. I'm Thirsty - p.64
4. A Cup of Grandmother's Advice - p.66

AUGUST

1. Let's Play Church - p.68
2. Life Can Be A Pain - p.70
3. I Want To Be Like Johnny - p.72
4. It's A Tradition - p.74
5. Get Your Six Iron Out - p.76

SEPTEMBER

1. Write Your Own Dash - p.78
2. Heroes - p.80
3. Why Aren't You Married? - p.82
4. What Are You Wearing? - p.84

OCTOBER

1. When The Doctor Is The Patient - p.86
2. Please Carry Me - p.88
3. Cave Dwellers - p.90
4. I'm 'Dopted - p.92

NOVEMBER

1. Are You Ladies Angels? - p.94
2. Fill Your Cup With God - p.96
3. What's Your Hurry? - p.98
4. I'm Starving - p.100

DECEMBER

1. Rescue Me - p.102
2. Cry With Him - p.104
3. Grace Is A Gift - p.106
4. All I Want For Christmas - p.108

Foreword
by Gary M. Bradley, Sr.

Cindi Bradley possesses a phenomenal insight into people. Undoubtedly, she was born with a great portion of this insight, because all of her life she has looked upon people with a spiritual eye. On various family trips, Cindi always made friends with others with whom she came into contact. At motels, amusement parks, playgrounds and parks, she quickly found out all about others who were there. Then, when the time came for us to leave, we could hear Cindi shout to them, "See you at the judgment!" It was amazing how she realized that, more than likely, she would never see those people again, yet she was so interested in learning all about their life history, where they were from, and where they were going. From this childhood characteristic, as she progressed to deeper relationships, Cindi has never lost her compassionate attitude. She cares about people. Her friends are dear to her and her loyalty to them is fierce. She cares about their spiritual well-being most of all.

Along with her insight into people, Cindi has developed and cultivated a superb insight into the Holy Scriptures. From the time she was the preacher in play church, she readily recognized practical applications for passages she knew. In adulthood, her applications proved to be true and faithful as she studied and applied them to life's situations. Cindi has used extensively her knowledge and understanding of the Scriptures in her lessons for women in various locations and settings. Her speaking ability has enhanced her understanding and contributed greatly to her presentations.

Cindi, as well, holds an insight into the need for motivation. She began to write her "Monday Thoughts" to share spiritual applications with her friends as each full week of work approached. This book is the composite of her applications. Cindi, knowing that many significant things were accomplished "early in the morning" by God's people, believed that spiritual strength would result from a few early morning sips of the Scriptures. Like our stimulating drink of choice in the morning, these sips of spirituality can motivate one into spending time with the Lord, stimulating further study of His word, thus propelling us into greater service for Him.

I am grateful and honored of the Lord to have been chosen to be Cindi's dad. She has been a joy to her entire family, and I love her dearly.

May God bless this book to His Glory!

Gary M. Bradley, Sr.

—⋘— **Preface** —⋙—

It's an incredible irony that I would select the title for this book, for many reasons. First of all, Monday! For so many, it's the most dreaded day of the week and the busiest part of our routine. Enjoying weekends the way I do, Monday mornings aren't always my favorite. I guess that's why years ago I began writing some "thoughts" on Sunday nights, attempting to steer my mind in a more spiritual direction. I figured it would be the best way to prepare for what lay ahead.

The idea that I would include coffee in my title is just nothing but hilarious. Every now and then just to be funny, my best friend, Sisty will ask me, "Can I get you a cup of coffee?" She knows it would be the first cup I've ever drank. She, on the other hand, has been drinking it since she was a child.

Fact is... I'm just not much of a coffee drinker.

Growing up in the Bradley household, one of the first words I would hear from Dad in the mornings was, "Is the coffee on?" That was in the days long before you could set a timer and the coffee pot would start on it's own. I remember seeing the coffee bubble up through the top of the pot as it perked. I also remember my grandparents boiling it on the stove and it being so hot that Pop Strickland drank his from a saucer.

Many, like Dad, can't begin their day without coffee. Every morning my co-workers arrive and it's almost like there's a fog in their head, with the first stop being the coffee pot. "Let me get my coffee and I'll be able to function." Like them, I can't function without my caffeine first thing in the morning, but I prefer mine cold in the form of a Coke or tea. Nothing feels worse than that headache I get when I miss my caffeine.

Even with everyone in my family being coffee drinkers, I just never learned to like it. I wish I did. It's aroma is so soothing, and it's so social. "Let's get a cup of coffee and we'll talk..." Everyone gathers and relaxes in the den or the living room, and what's in the middle of that room? A COFFEE table.

It's so accessible. Office break rooms, waiting rooms and even Sunday School classrooms at church have coffee pots. Nowadays you can't drive down many streets in most major American cities without passing a Starbucks. That's a company I wish I had bought stock in some years ago. Not only can you get a basic cup of coffee but they've become very creative with their beverages. *"I'll have a grande mocha latte decaf skinny soy macchiota mumbo jumbo Americano.... to go, please".*

There are many things I like about coffee. I love the smell when it's brewing. It has such a distinct aroma, and once it is detected, there is no doubt that it's coffee. Anytime I walk in Starbucks or Barney's or any other coffee shop, I sniff it all in and out comes an "ahhhhhhhh".... how appealing.

There are some aspects of our lives that are much like my association with coffee. Some areas in life are not what we had in mind or they just don't meet our expectations. Oh, some things look so good. The aroma is so appetizing and tempting. But, when you pour yourself a big cup, all you taste is disappointment. You can, like me, even try to change it and maybe then it's acceptable. Add some sugar to sweeten it up or better yet, use the stuff in the pink, blue or yellow packets and make it sweet with "artificial" ingredients.

Boy, there's a sermon right there. Make it smooth with some cream or better yet, different flavors of cream. My friend, Melisa likes the cream that tastes like Almond Joy candy bars. I've tried all of that, but to no avail.

Maybe I just need to accept the fact that unless I like coffee by now, nothing is going to change. It's just a taste that I'll never acquire. Accepting that fact includes that I quit trying to change it and make it something that it's not.

Maybe I need to accept the fact that some things in life aren't what I expect them to be. I can try to change it but "it is what it is." Changing my expectations is a possibility, or perhaps not expecting too much is another thought.

Or like the apostle Paul, maybe I just need a good lesson in being content.

But... I still don't like coffee.

Now by all means, you go ahead and enjoy your morning cup, even have a second - and while you're sipping, enjoy a story, from my heart to yours.

Warm Wishes,

Cindi Bradley

Note:.
I originally wrote each of these stories on Sunday nights and e-mailed them to friends and family under the title "Monday Thoughts." They typically arrived in the reader's in-box on Monday mornings, and became a regular part of their weekly start-up. I hope you enjoy reading one of the weekly devotionals each Monday morning, and that you find encouragement that will last all week long.

JANUARY · WEEK ONE

Are You Warm Enough?   *Ephesians* 3:20

    The wind was howling outside and the temperature had dropped far below the average that we normally have for January in Alabama. Occasionally, we dip down into those frigid temps but, for the most part, we have rather mild winters. Anytime I walk outside on days when it's beyond cold I allow my mind to mentally go to a warm sandy beach with crystal clear waters.

    "Are you warm enough?" The question came from Dad as he walked past my room and he wanted to make sure I wasn't freezing. Just after moving to Huntsville, I lived with my parents until I could get a place of my own. How comforting it was to be home on a cold winter night.

    When I went to bed, I pulled my down comforter almost to the top of my head. Being thankful had just crossed my mind as I felt the warmth coming from the vent just above me. When you combine the down comforter, gas heat from the vent and my favorite flannel pajamas - there was no way any cool draft was getting in through the bedroom windows.

"Yes sir, I'm fine. Thank you. Good night."

    As I woke Sunday morning, the wind continued its howl and the temperature was even lower than when I went to bed. The ground had a slight dusting of snow making the leaves look like a dry bowl of Frosted Mini Wheats. The winter made the grass a dirty brown then the dusting of snow made it look just like a bowl of cereal.

    Dad held my coat as I put my arms through the sleeves. We were stepping out the door for church when he commented, "You might want to make sure you have your gloves and something around your face. Find you a hat - you know 60% of body heat escapes from your head. That wind is brutal."

Once again, he was making sure I was warm. He had already gone outside and cranked the car so it would be warm enough for Mom and me. A thoughtful thing to do but it's also a way to motivate us to hurry up so we can leave.

At our house, Dad is the protector and provider. He makes sure there's plenty of heat in the house and that we have what we need to stay warm. He's had that job well over 50 years now and I've got to say, he's the best I've ever known with the job. Even during the years I lived miles away he would call, "Honey, is your heat running OK. Make sure your car has enough anti-freeze and your tires are at the proper inflation." It's all part of being a Dad.

Our heavenly Father does the same thing. He provides warmth and protects us against the elements of winter, but also against a cold sinful world. With that in mind, I ask you again, "Are you warm enough? Are you allowing God to wrap His arms of warmth and protection around you and keep you warm?

Sin, selfishness and pride wilt our heart and causes our faith to become very cold. It doesn't take much to recognize this type of heart. It's usually accompanied with anger, bitterness, malice or it belongs to someone who is just plain mean. No fancy word for it - it's just meanness! Those are cold adjectives and as I write them I picture in my mind the limbs on the tree that are brittle and layered with cold, thick ice. It's almost painful to even touch them and a mere tug will break them into pieces.

While sin might have taken its toll on our lives, the love of God can quickly melt the coldest of hearts. The forgiving blood of Christ provides a thermal blanket of warmth and the amazing fact is, He never withdraws His love - no matter how bad I mess things up.

Cold, sleepless nights brought on by worry and doubt can become warm and cozy comforts of sleep. There is no better sleeping pill than the assurance of God's love. It is our loving Father asking you, "Are you warm enough?" Keep in mind, He's not promising that there will never be cold nights again. He's not promising that you'll never have to face the wind.

He is promising an undying, unconditional, always faithful love that provides far more warmth than you could EVER dream of.

One last time I ask you...

"Are you warm enough?"

My Father wants to know.

JANUARY - WEEK TWO

I'm Right Here  Proverbs 3:5

The hallway was dark and scary but it was only a few steps from my bedroom to Mom and Dad's. Anything in the dark was scary for me at the age of 6. I had been in bed a few hours but woke up not really understanding what was going on. I was so cold but yet my hair, pajamas and pillow were wet with sweat. My throat felt like I had swallowed steak knives and the ringing in my ears was almost unbearable.

Those are common ailments that come on a six year old at any time and they had definitely hit me. I tiptoed into Mom and Dad's room and felt my way in the dark to Mom's side of the bed. She was sleeping so soundly until she heard the frail whisper, "Mom. Mommy."

Her deep sleep was immediately disrupted and in a concerned but startled voice she asked, "What is it?" Instinctively, she placed her hands on my face then put her cheek up against mine. That's the maternal thermometer and its accuracy is better than anything you can get at the drug store.

"Gary, she's burning up." Dad finally stirred a little and rolled over to see what was going on. He opened his eyes a little wider to see me sitting on the side of the bed. "Her temp is well over 102 degrees and we've got to do something." I had no idea what time the clock read but it was well after midnight.

Dad found the aspirin and Mother filled the bathtub with cool water. The aspirin didn't stay down long nor did any other fluids they tried. At that point they knew it was time to consult a doctor.

We were living in Chattanooga at the time and had not been there very long. We had not become established with a local pediatrician so our physician sources were limited. Thankfully, there was a good friend from church that was doing his residency at Erlanger Hospital. He worked all the time so the chances of him being available that particular Friday night were pretty good.

Dad called the number for his beeper and just as we hoped, he was at the hospital. I still remember Dad's tired voice, "George, thanks for calling me back. Cindi's fever is sky high and her throat is like raw meat. Can you help us?" Before I could even think, Dad scooped me up, put me in the car and to Erlanger's Emergency Room he drove.

There weren't many places more educational for a six year old than the ER at Erlanger on a Friday night. I felt like I was about ten feet in the air as my Dad carried me down the hall. When you're six years old, someone 6'3" feels more like you're being carried by Goliath. I rested my head on his shoulder and he tried to secure me in his arms as he walked quickly down the hall.

The nurse showed us to a room and we waited for Dr. George. For some odd reason, they made me take my clothes off and they put me in this silly gown that had no back to it. What's up with that? Then, they made me sit on this table that had to have spent a tremendous amount of time in a large cooler or freezer. A cold table and a backless gown do not bode well on this body.

The nurse had taken my temperature, and just as Mom had predicted - it was over 102.

With fever that high, it causes an ache that spreads all over the body. Having someone touch you and mash your belly is twice as uncomfortable. For years, Mom and Dad had taught me to never put anything sharp in my ears. This genius level guy who had spent most of his life in school walks in the room and what's the first thing he does? Puts this sharp light right in the hole of my ear. Then, he takes a popsicle stick and mashes it on my tongue halfway down my throat. He wanted an "ahhhhhhh" but what he got was a "GAG!" He pulled his stethoscope (out of the same freezer that stored the table I was sitting on, I guess) and placed it on my bear chest. Another "hmmmmmmmmmmmmmm" comes from him.

Following all of that, he goes into some medical explanation and it all sounded Greek to me but I did catch the last words, "She'll need a shot and then we'll prescribe some other meds." It was AMAZING how quickly I began to feel better. It was a miracle! That doctor in his residency was truly a genius. I didn't understand a word he said but there was no doubt in my mind that by sticking that light in my ear and cramming that popsicle stick down my throat- I WAS HEALED!

My squirming became very obvious because I heard the pop of Daddy's fingers, "Cindi, be still!" He knew the thought of making a run for it had already crossed my mind. I hated shots! Anytime I got one, my screams started before the nurse filled the syringe. It always burned me up because the nurse would lie every time with that infamous statement: "NOW THIS WON'T HURT!" Yeah, right!

There I was on that freezing cold table feeling like death on a Ritz cracker and now this huge needle is about to stick the fleshiest part of my "sit down". The tears had already welled up and Dad's hand was red from me squeezing it. The nurse had to pat my leg ever so slightly, "OK, Baby, you've got to be still now."

The scream was about to belt from my mouth when I felt something on my shoulders just above my head. It was Daddy's hands on my shoulders and his whispering voice in my ear, "It's OK. I'm right here. She's not going to hurt you."

That nurse could have hit me with a machete and I would have stayed right there because my Daddy said, "It's alright. I'm right here."

Do you feel God's hands on you? Life gets pretty scary. Sometimes our greatest fears become reality. Sooner or later we all face our midnights and it's our faith that allows us to feel the mighty hands of our heavenly Father on our shoulders and hear His voice tell us, "It's OK. TRUST ME!"

- **When the test comes back and the doctor says "CANCER!" Trust Him.**
- **When you've lost your job and have no idea how bills will be paid - Trust Him.**
- **When the one who promised to stay with you for the rest of your life has turned to another - Trust Him.**

I'll never be able to answer the "whys." I don't know why Moms and Dads give up and tear their family apart. I don't know why people have to suffer with cancer. I don't know why it seems like people who have no respect for God seem to prosper so well.

What I do know is, if I trust God and lean not on my own understanding. (Ps. 37:3)

He'll make it plain one day. ONE DAY.

JANUARY - WEEK THREE

Wo 🍃 Ruth 1:16

A story written in 1998 by my Mother, Bobbie Bradley

She was forty-eight, I was eighteen. I had already figured that out, along with the fact that she trusted me unquestionably with her only son whom she loved "better than dirt", as she used to say.

"Come here and see our new daughter," she called.

As I sat before the mirror in my high ceilinged bedroom in my white organdy gown, she and her husband came into the room. He was shy, but she talked for both of them for a moment, and then they walked next door to the church where I was to be married. I never gave a thought that hot August day to what she was going to mean in my life. In a whirlwind of rice and excitement, I and my new husband ran in our shiny new shoes to our shiny old car and set out on a journey that has lasted now for forty years... after all, she was only my mother-in-law.

Six weeks later, after a trip to her doctor, I found myself in her softly-lit bedroom, crying:

"We're going to have a baby! What'll I do? What'll we do? I have to work; he has to finish college! What are we going to do with a baby? Besides, this baby's due the last of May and we only got married in August. How did this happen?"

"Well THIS surely isn't a virgin birth! It's not a question of what you'll do with a baby, it's what that baby will do and become. You will love him! And another thing, I don't want to hear anything about that baby having to adjust to your schedule! You'll just adjust to him when he gets here. The Lord will take care of things."

"How do you know it's going to be a boy?"...after all, she was just my mother-in-law!

"I just know, that's all."

And she did - just like she knew just about everything. I didn't even pick out a girl's name.

So the days and years came and went, and she rocked and crooned to each of my three babies while I watched from my bed, (quote) "getting a good night's rest so that I would have strength to get through the next day."

I never wondered how she got through the next day. She went to school every morning at eight and didn't come back until four. Yet, there she was every afternoon, every night, always hearing the softest cries of the little ones before I did, nurturing them - and me.

"What's wrong?" Her voice would be low and stern on the other end of the phone.

6

"What do you mean, "what's wrong," I would ask. After all, she was just my mother-in-law.

"Something's wrong. What is it?"

It's then that I would break down and tell her that we had just returned from the emergency room with whichever of the children had gone that time, and in five minutes she would be walking through the back door.

Or, when I called her and said, "I need you," she packed her car with clothes and food (and her maid) and came tearing to our house 150 miles away to take care of my children as my frail little grandmother lay dying. She hit the door in spike heels, a new "pant suit", reeking of Chanel No. 5, ready to take charge. To this day, I don't know how she got that much food ready so fast and that many clothes in that car, much less how she talked that maid into coming with her.

"Hewwo."
"Cindi, let me speak to Wo."
"Mommy, Wo didn't make us go to church. We played."
"Wo, did you take the children to church?"
 (After all, it's Wednesday night, and Cindi is prone to making up stuff)
"Noooo, I didn't."
"What?"

"I said, I didn't take them. All these children know and have ever known is church, church, church. They even PLAY church. So I kept them home. (There was a long pause and a sigh). Besides that, I didn't think Irma would feel comfortable there. (her maid was African American and a new christian), and I wasn't about to leave her. What would that say to her, us traipsing off to church and leaving her? So, we had church here. We had Bible stories and Cindi preached. You know, she's going to preach better than her daddy someday." It was 1965 - the height of the racial crisis. She was right - she **was** my mother-in-law.

"I'll be there this afternoon. My flight arrives at 2:55." It was 1974, and her voice was firm. A judge had decided our foster baby should return to her birth parents. She was our heart from the time she was three months old, and now, after three years, she was gone.
"OK, we'll be there to pick you up, Wo."
"No, you'll stay home; both of you are having walking-around-nervous breakdowns. I'll take a cab."
"Wo, they just came and got her. Gary's about to go crazy, calling the school to check on the children, running around like he's lost his mind."
"Bobbie, you'll both get through this. Sure, she was your heart, but her mother will take care of her now. You'll see. The Lord will take care of things. He'll help her - and you."

He did - and she was right. She **was** my mother-in-law...my friend. *(continued)*

Wo (cont.)  Ruth 1:16

(cont.) "You've been the best daughter-in-law I could have ever wanted," she whispered from her bed in 1992, "and such a good mother, too. I want to tell you that, because I'll be leaving soon."

"Oh, Otis, I love you", was all that I could get out, as I sat on the wicker stool beside her.

We both knew she was leaving. Her breathing was shallow, but her intuition was deep, and as our eyes met and held, each knew the thoughts of the other.

I was her daughter-in-law, wife of her only son. She was Wo, my friend, my mentor, who possessed the uncanny talent for reading my mind, for saying the right thing, for saying nothing, for knowing exactly what I needed, and for doing it. She could command the attention of a room full of people; yet she could communicate with babies, old folks and special children (whom she taught for years). She had a rapport with doctors, nurses, preachers, elders, and especially pregnant women, somehow knowing when you were "going into labor" before you had a pain.

In some mysterious way, she felt the pain of others and did all she could to ease it. She would teach school all day, come home, fry up chickens for supper (always extra to send to anyone who needed it), give a shower at her house, and feed and cuddle my babies into the wee hours of the morning. She could sing like a bird, talk for hours about her favorite movie stars and the latest hits of her country music singers, and offer solutions to ALL the church's problems - in one night. She knew more people who needed help than anybody else, and, usually, she had already helped them before anybody could figure out who they were or what they needed! She loved teas, luncheons, "good-looking clothes", perfume, pink, chicken salad, Psalm 23, Proverbs 31, good singing and preaching at church, all the flowers she could get and teenagers.

She knew my heart and she built a bridge of love through her faith in me and through her encouragement from her heart to mine. She communicated confidence, never minimized fears, shed tears of concern, and always expressed high expectations. She affirmed positively, saying, "You can do it. You're right," or to my husband, "Listen to her, she's right!" or "She knows what she's doing."

She always made me feel that I was the best hostess, best mother, best preacher's wife that had ever tried and that anything I did was "beau...teee...ful, dahlin"...unless we ran out of her favorite drink, "Dr. Peppah."

During good times or bad, all I needed to hear was, "Wo's here." and everything was all right. Now, Wo's not here, but where Wo is I hope to go one day, and, just as

Ruth followed Naomi, I will follow Wo, softly saying:

"Whither thou goest, I will go."

After all, she's my mother-in-law...*my best friend.*

Mother and Daddy's Wedding Day in 1957. Mom and Pop Strickland on Mother's right; Wo and Grandaddy on Daddy's left

1990 - Wo's 80th birthday and her granddaughters Garen, Lisa, and me

JANUARY · WEEK FOUR

Be Found In Him *Luke 15*

Have you ever lost an item around the house and spent a lot of time searching for it? I am notorious for losing my car keys at least three times a week. What's really embarrassing to admit is, they are usually right in front of me, or at least located in a very obvious place. You may call it a "senior moment."

One Sunday morning I was almost late to church because I couldn't find my car keys. I immediately went into a panic searching all over my house for them because I hate being late to church. Besides, at Mayfair if you're not there at least ten minutes before worship starts, you don't get YOUR parking place or YOUR seat. Thankfully, my keys appeared before my eyes...on the dining room table right where I tossed them when I got home from work Saturday night.

One Saturday morning, I met Mom and Dad for breakfast at Gibson's (best biscuits in town, other than my Mom's) and I arrived early to get us a table. Mom came in as Dad parked the car. A few minutes later Dad walked through the entrance and looked over the restaurant to see where we were sitting. He had the funniest look on his face. His eyes scanned all over the room and finally Mom waved her hand - we were right under his nose.

Sometimes we make things so difficult, but in reality, they're not. We search for fulfillment in our lives and we search for happiness and we search for peace and we extend that search for many years. The pain and the cost of our search is more extensive than words can describe. We expect that search to be so extensive and involved when, actually, it's right under our nose.

Newborn baby Drew Kimbrough enjoys his first Gibson's biscuit

Some of us have worn ourselves out searching for whatever it is will fill the emptiness in our lives. How ridiculous would it have been for me to continue to search for my keys after I found them? I mean, that's down right stupid. Yet, some of us are so consumed with the search itself and consumed with the desire of finding something better, that we keep digging and we keep grasping and we keep reaching for more, when all we need is right there in our hands.

Why? Why do we put ourselves through that?

Years ago, I had a friend tell me that the reason she drank so much alcohol in college was because she was so empty inside. I asked her if the alcohol ever filled the void and of course, the answer was no. Satan has deceived a countless number of people and made them believe that those pills will eventually make them feel good all the time. Maybe it's a relationship that they have no business being in but yet they've bought the lie and are convinced true happiness and true fulfillment is found in that person.

Then there's the person who says:

"Just a little more money…yeah, everything would be perfect if I had more money."

When is it ever enough?

Eventually, this search wears you down and you become emotionally, physically and yes, spiritually exhausted. People who are young look much older than their true age because the search has worn them down.

Jesus said: *"Come to me and I'll give you REST."* (Matthew 11:28-30)

The fulfillment, completeness and yes, the peace that we all so desperately want, is found in Christ. Not in a bottle; not in a needle; not in a pill; not even in a person.

Some of us have sat on a church pew since we were riding a stick horse, but yet we keep searching for what's right there in our hands. Even a pew Bible has the answer.

Jesus did the searching for us.

Now let yourself be found in **Him.**

JANUARY - WEEK FIVE

Rescue The Perishing *Proverbs 24:11*

One of the things that has always amazed me in the scriptures is how God never needed some ideal candidate to be His rescue person. Think about it - the people He called on to do great things were not necessarily ones that would have been picked by any of us. Throughout the Bible, some of the most influential men and women of God had questionable credentials.

In Judges 6, God needed a rescue person. Gideon is not the one we would have picked. He would have never been any blue chip recruit or made any team's draft board. He would not have been General Schwarzkopf's choice to lead troops in the Gulf War. He was the "least of his family" (verse 15) and quick to come up with excuses when God called him.

The Bible (from The Message) tells us that God came to Gideon and said, "Go in this strength you have and save Israel out of Midian's hand."

"ME?" I can picture Gideon looking over his shoulders and thinking, "You talking to me?" "How and with what could I ever save Israel? Look at me. My clan's the weakest in Manneseh and I'm the runt of the litter." God said to him, "I'll be with you. Believe me, you'll defeat Midian as one man."

In Chapter 7 we read of God reducing Gideon's army by thousands but yet, even out numbered, he still defeats the Midianites - just as God told him he would. In a matter of days, Gideon went from "hiding wimp" to "God's warrior."

Peter made his living as a fisherman and quite frankly, he wasn't very good at it. In Luke 5, he is putting away his nets after a very unsuccessful fishing trip. While putting away the fishing gear, Jesus came to him and the others and told them to launch their boat back on the water and try again.

"What?" (I'm paraphrasing here). Peter tried to reason with Jesus and explain, "We've been fishing all night and we've not caught a thing. But, because you say so, we'll go out again."

I bet you know the story. Peter and the rest launched their boat and put their nets where Jesus told them to. Those nets filled with fish so fast, they began to break. He had to call others to come help because the boat was beginning to sink. Peter was so amazed by this that he fell at the feet of Jesus probably in a pile of fish and said, "Go away from me. I'm a sinful man."

Jesus told Peter to get up from the fish and not to be afraid. "Peter, from now on you will catch men." Luke goes on to say that he pulled in his boat and left EVERYTHING to follow Him. That always impressed me with Peter. He was a fisherman by trade and he had just experienced the most amazing day of his entire career. Never before had he caught so many fish. Think of the money that all those fish would have brought in. But, he was willing to leave it all and follow Jesus. That same foul mouth fisherman became God's spokesman on the day of Pentecost.

During my years in Chattanooga, I met a man who is an amazing servant of God.

His name is Dr. Todd Rudolph and he, along with his wife Michelle, are dear friends of mine. When I met them in 2000, little did I know they had gone through a storm that few could have survived.

It was on May 15, 1999 that the lie Todd Rudolph had been living was exposed. Todd had gone through medical school and was about to complete his residency. He and Michelle were living day to day, hoping one day he would be the doctor he dreamed of being. With a three year old son and a one year old daughter, finances were tight.

Todd's instructor confronted him, placed a specimen cup on the desk and demanded he take a drug test. The excuses fell from Todd's mouth immediately and his nervous talk incriminated him even more. Todd failed that drug test. That instructor looked Todd in the eye and said, "You're a drug addict and an alcoholic. Get some help or lose it all."

Todd got the help he needed. After three months of rehab he wiped the slate clean, finished his residency and became that doctor he always dreamed of being. He proved to Michelle and his children there is something far greater than drugs or alcohol. It didn't happen over night, but one day at a time, he poured himself into Christ - not into a bottle.

Hearing Todd's testimony from the pulpit at East Brainerd Church of Christ was life changing for many of us. It was so obvious that Todd's message hit home as some in attendance were struggling with their own addictions. Some (like my family) had someone they dearly loved that was battling with drugs and alcohol. Somebody had finally removed the mask and showed publicly how God cleanses all sins.

I had no idea this man of God had almost thrown it all away. How could God use a man that was tempted to drink? How could God use a man that for so long had to go to a rehab center and learn to live without drugs? Believe me, for many years God has placed His hands on Todd Rudolph's shoulders and told him, "GO".

Todd continues to answer that call. Not long after sharing his story from the pulpit, Todd led a class teaching the 12 step program. Never before had I ever seen a more effective ministry. I saw Todd and Michelle bring more people to the Lord than any other outreach I've ever seen.

 I love Todd and Michelle Rudolph. Todd has been clean for many years but not just from his addiction to drugs and alcohol but also to his addiction to Satan's lies. I love how Todd loves God's people and how he wants them to know a life with Jesus and a walk with Him. I love how Todd continues to tell me, "Cindi, I am nothing, but God is EVERYTHING!"

You don't think God can use you? Think again.

God used a wimp like Gideon, a foul-mouthed fisherman like Peter, a strung out med student named Todd and yes, He can do amazing things with you.

FEBRUARY - WEEK ONE

We All Need Open Heart Surgery *Matt. 6:21*

In all of my years of working at Huntsville Hospital, I've seen that each day is different and the only thing you can expect, is the unexpected. Another way of putting it: THERE'S NEVER A DULL MOMENT.

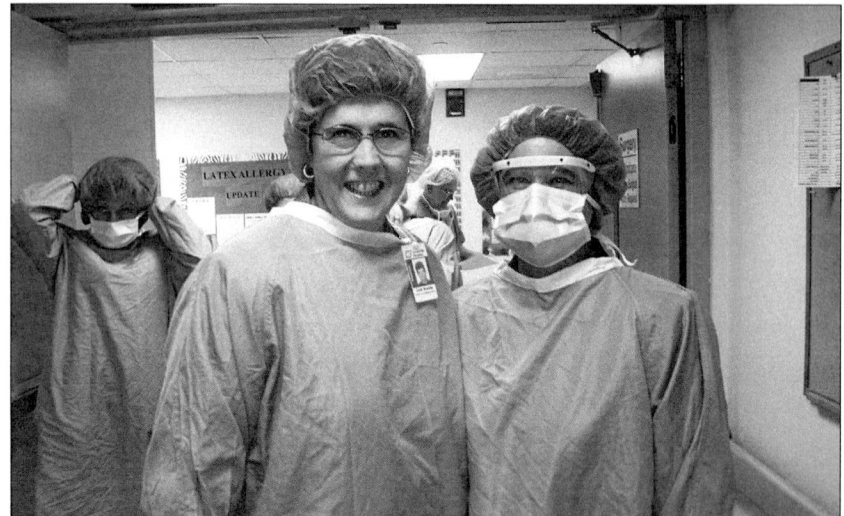

The hospital hosted a session for local executives who were participating in a leadership program with the Huntsville Chamber of Commerce. They familiarized themselves with the healthcare industry in Huntsville and that included a tour of our hospital.

I was honored and thrilled to be part of the program as a tour guide. Various groups were assigned certain departments of the hospital and they were allowed to see areas that most visitors are not allowed to see. Some went to the Neo-Natal Intensive Care Unit, while others watched the latest technology in robotic surgery.

My group toured the Cardiovascular Operating Room (CVOR) and learned the ins and outs of open heart surgery. We dressed in the surgical wardrobe and got to wash our hands like a real surgeon. Some of the nurses were on hand to demonstrate various procedures such as harvesting veins from a patient's leg. No, they didn't demonstrate on one of us but rather they have a "dummy" that they use to practice on and train. I remember not too long ago, a patient would have a huge incision in his/her leg for this procedure but now technology allows the cut to be very minimal.

Another employee showed us the heart and lung machine and how it basically breathes for the patient and keeps him/her alive during the procedure. I had to chuckle when I saw the surgical instruments used because they looked like something a mechanic would use for a car. About 45 tweezers, clamps and what looked like pliers were all lined up ready for the surgeon to do his work. There was even a drill that looked like something you would buy at Home Depot, used to open the chest.

From there, we stood at the window and watched as the cardiologist concentrated on what is cited as the most invasive surgery a person can undergo. There it was - a person's heart. The very muscle that pumps life-sustaining blood throughout our bodies. The muscle that without it, none of us can live. I had no clue who the patient was nor could I even tell if it was a male or a female. It didn't matter. In my head, I prayed for that person and I prayed for the physician as he made the repairs.

I rarely have times when I'm speechless, but I had to ask the nurse, "So, the doctor is actually looking inside that person's heart and seeing all parts of it?" After the affirmative answer, we watched a little longer and then exited the CVOR amazed at what we had seen. Not being a nurse or a doctor, it doesn't take much to fascinate me with things like this. I've not been able to get that vision out of my head, nor do I think I ever will.

Knowing the importance of the heart in our physical bodies, I began to think of the importance of the heart in our spiritual lives. Reading through the Bible, so much emphasis is placed on the heart. It brings this question to my mind: What if someone could see inside of MY heart? What would they see? Would I be hesitant to let them look? Are there things that I thought I had hidden, but my actions tell otherwise?

Is there a chamber in my heart of humility? Paul wrote in Philippians 2 of how we are to have the mind of Christ (or heart - same thing) and live a life of humility as He did. My friend, Phyllis Watson has this kind of heart. Anytime I'm around Phyllis, she has the mind of Christ and wants so badly to live for Him. I don't want Phyllis's football heart (she's an Auburn fan) but I see Jesus in her life and I KNOW what's in her heart.

Is there a chamber in my heart of unselfishness? Do I do for others and treat others as I would want to be treated? My friend, Ann Minor, has one of the most unselfish hearts of anyone I know. She gives and expects nothing in return because she loves people and cares so much. I wish I could be more like that.

Is there a chamber in my heart for purity and holiness? My Aunt Rose Turner corners the market on that one in my book. Not only can she quote Philippians 4:8 - she *lives* it.

I ask these questions because what's in my heart is who I really am. What I care about; what I talk about; what I spend my money on; who I spend my time with - that's a reflection of what's in my heart. Paul wrote in Romans 12:1-3, that since Jesus is in our hearts, we need to TRANSFORM that and put the life of Jesus on display in our own lives.

It all starts when we allow The Great Physician to turn our hearts. Maybe we need to replace some valves. Maybe we need to clean out some arteries.

Whatever it takes. He's ready for the procedure.

"Turn my heart O, Lord like rivers of water - Turn my heart O, Lord by your hand
Til my whole life flows in the river of your Spirit - And my name brings honor to the Lamb"

FEBRUARY · WEEK TWO

What's In Your Heart? *I Thess. 4:1-5*

During my years in Birmingham, I worked for a company that was located in a part of town called Inverness. It was a very scenic area with beautiful houses, lots of trees and a man-made lake that flowed near a beautiful golf course. Our office was located on the sixth floor overlooking that lake.

Many afternoons I'd find myself daydreaming, looking out over that lake and wishing I was in a small boat soaking the sun. Just outside the window of my office, there was the most gorgeous tree with its roots right by that water. Every now and then, on the days that weather and time permitted, I'd take my lunch and sit by that tree. The scenery was just beautiful.

I loved that tree. The circumference was so big and round and it stood far taller than any other tree on that property. There were lots of other trees all over the woods but that tree stood out more, at least to me. My co-workers used to tease me about being so possessive with "my tree." I'd point out the beauty of the tree to them and they readily agreed it was a place of comfort and shade.

Then one morning it happened. I saw the true colors of "my tree." I saw what "my tree" was really made of. A freak of nature hit Birmingham on March 12, 1993. Many probably don't even have to stop and think to recall the event.

Yep - THE BIRMINGHAM BLIZZARD!

The snow began to fall around 7:00 that Friday night and by 6:00 Saturday morning, 18 inches had fallen to the ground. It was the first time in my life I had seen lightening and heard thunder during a snowstorm. The wind howled and the snow piled up quickly.

The entire state had experienced snow. Even as far south as Mobile, things were at a stand still because, yes, it had snowed. There's been a joke for many years in the state of Alabama regarding the three things we fear the most: Snow, tornadoes, and a Yankee with a U-Haul! Snow paralyzes the state of Alabama.

Things were completely shut down in Birmingham on Saturday, Sunday and Monday. Schools closed, offices closed, roads iced over - no one was going anywhere, except in an emergency. By Tuesday, we had all dug out and finally our cars were past the driveway. It took a little while but I made it to the office along with many of my co-workers. Much of the Inverness area looked like a war zone with trees down and limbs covering the streets. Slowly but surely electricity was being restored and thankfully, our office was up and going.

As I sat at my desk and began organizing some things, I glanced out the window. Most of the trees had endured the storm but a lot of limbs and branches had covered the ground. That's when I noticed it. The tree I loved and admired so much was gone.

I grabbed my coat and walked through the woods to take a look. Three-fourths of the tree was lying in the shallow waters of the lake. The wind had completely uprooted that tree and it looked as if it broke like a cheap toothpick. That's when I noticed what "my tree" was truly made of. The inside of that tree was corroded and rotten. My face cringed as I looked because what I thought was so beautiful and perfect was actually nasty on the inside. The roots were small and it's a wonder the tree lived as long as it did. All of the other trees that were not as beautiful on the outside, endured the storm because obviously, they had solid roots and a strong heart on the inside.

What about us? What's our make-up? What are we made of? Do we look so beautiful on the outside and make incredible impressions on people and have them convinced that we have it all together? But, when real life occurs we fall like a feather in the wind.

Peter addressed this with women in I Peter 3:4 when he wrote that beauty doesn't come from fancy hair, gold jewelry and fine clothes. But, it comes from within you - the beauty of a gentle and quiet spirit and purity. I'm paraphrasing there.

Now, my grandmother Bradley used to say, "A little paint on the barn never hurt anybody." She's right. The Lord isn't telling us to ignore our appearance. On the other hand, far too many of us put more attention on masking who we really are and hiding our character with outward appearance rather than cleaning up the inside.

One day the inside is exposed. What's on the inside eventually comes out for the whole world to see. Satan is just waiting for the most opportune time when he can do the most damage to expose us. Maybe others are already seeing it and just not saying anything. Maybe we've got a lot of people fooled and we think we're truly getting by with the whole lie. The truth is, the only person we are fooling is ourselves.

The commercial on TV asks, "What's in your wallet?"

I'm asking, *"What's in your heart?"*

FEBRUARY - WEEK THREE

Bridge Builders   *Galatians 6:10*

Blessings to each of you from the beautiful shores of the Gulf of Mexico. As I write these thoughts, I am looking out over the water and watching others walk along the beach in Destin, Florida. My friend, Melisa and I escaped reality for a few days and enjoyed some time together.

Destin is truly one of my favorite places on this earth. It's filled with memories and warm thoughts for me as I've vacationed here so many times with family and friends. I can still picture my nephews, Tripp, Will and Clay as little guys running up and down this very beach. Not too far from where I sit is the very swimming pool where I taught Tripp how to swim.

I think I've spent more time in Destin with Melisa than any friend I have. She's my favorite "Beach Buddy" and we share a kindred spirit when it comes to the beach.

We have our rituals when we come to Destin...

- The Donut Hole is a ritual.
- Dewey Destin's Seafood is a ritual.
- Falling asleep in our beach chairs is a ritual.

And many mornings, I carry out one of my favorite rituals - driving over the Destin Bridge. Kind of a strange ritual but at some point during my visit I have to drive over "my bridge."

It amuses Melisa when I call it "my bridge" but it's my favorite. It's one of the most beautiful areas of Destin as you can see the pass - where the bay and the gulf meet. The jetties line the shore and it's fun to watch the boats of all sizes go through the pass and travel under the bridge. I've looked through my Bible and a concordance and I can't seem to find any reference to a bridge.

There are tunnels that have been named; also caves, mountains, hills, rivers and seas...but no mention of a bridge. On the other hand there are many human bridges throughout the 66 books of the Bible. A bridge connects two opposite sides and brings them together. It allows you to cross a gap where otherwise you could not reach the other side.

Moses was a bridge. By delivering God's commandments to the children of Israel, he bridged the gap between God and His people. He led them to the Promised Land. The Apostle Paul was a bridge as he traveled throughout the land spreading the Gospel and establishing churches everywhere he went. Once he persecuted Christians and took the lives of those who claimed the name of Jesus as Lord and Savior...until he saw the light, so to speak, on the road to Damascus. Of course, the ultimate example of a bridge is our Lord and Savior, Jesus Christ. Never has anyone bridged the gap and connected us to our Heavenly Father like he does.

So, what about my life? Is my life a bridge?

Peter writes in I Peter 2:9 that we are a royal priesthood. We're all Priests. The word "priest" is translated to mean "bridgebuilder". Is my life a ministry? Is my example one that bridges the gap between a lost world and God? Is my life a path for people to cross over to something better; where they will find peace and eternal life?

It takes time to build a bridge. It takes planning and it takes patience. The architect who designs a bridge must use special materials and somehow build support beams that cannot be weakened by strong waters, winds or storms. God is the perfect architect in our lives and by following His plan, we bridge the gap to a once hopeless world. My life can be that bridge for people I come in contact with daily who are hurting and need the kind of strength that only God can give.

As I drive over "my bridge" in Destin,
I admire the beauty of the water and the glow of the sky.
I can only hope as people watch my actions and see my life,
the gap is bridged - and the beauty of our Father is seen.

It's what we're all called to do.

FEBRUARY · WEEK FOUR

Where Y'all From? *Philippians 4:8*

Who says the beach is only for summer days? NOT ME! That's why my best friend, Melisa and I give no hesitation to throwing our beach chairs in the car and running down to Destin, Florida even in the dead of winter. One February weekend was an ideal time to celebrate her upcoming birthday and relax a day or two. We managed to pick a weekend when God decided He was tired of cold, snowy, dreary days as well.

February 19th felt more like May 19th as we sat in our chairs and soaked the sun. No need for a sweater, no need for hats and gloves, no need to warm up the car before you pull out of the drive - the only thing we didn't pack enough of was sunscreen. Swimsuits, shorts, T-shirts and flip-flops were the attire of the day. Amazingly, children ran to the water with their boogie boards and gave no thought to jumping right in as if it were the middle of July.

While in Destin, Melisa and I never have to spend a lot of time deciding where to eat dinner. Dewey Destin's Seafood is our absolute favorite restaurant not only for the great scenery, but for the absolute best seafood anywhere on the Gulf coast. Dewey is a "local" so his seafood is from the area and is very fresh. Nothing fancy about the ambiance - but that's what we like about it. You sit at a picnic table and your food comes in a plastic basket. If you want more sweet tea, you get up and get it yourself.

After a restful day of soaking in the warm sunshine, we made our way down Highway 98 to the Destin Harbor. We had discussed previously how we wanted to get there in time to watch the sun go down over the Choctawatchee Bay and let me tell you, that's a sight that can never be put into words. Watching that has got to confuse any atheist. Simply BEAUTIFUL - and based on the number of people who were facing the bay, they appreciated the beauty as much as we did.

Dewey Destin's "Grouper Cheeks" - delicious, and possibly the world's freshest fish

Melisa and I walked out on the pier and tried to take as many pictures as we could before the sun dropped beyond the horizon. While standing there, a lady commented on the scenery and asked me if we had ever been there before. I answered her and ended up striking up a conversation. She was from up north - a snow bird and forgoing a long cold winter in Michigan for the sunny skies of Florida. I was wearing a shirt I had bought as a souvenir from New York so she asked, "You girls from New York?" I almost had to laugh and respectfully answered, "No ma'am."

She chuckled and said, "Well, you sure don't sound like you're from New York. *Where are you from?*" In a slow southern drawl I jokingly answered, "MICHIGAN!"

But, she knew I was being silly. *"She lives in Birmingham and I'm from Huntsville."*

Then she said, *"You didn't have to tell me. I was going to guess Alabama because you couldn't pass for a Yankee if you tried."* My accent gave me away. No way I could convince her that I hailed from anywhere else but the Deep South.

Later that night, I recalled that conversation and was reminded of a time in the Bible when an accent blew Peter's cover. Remember when Jesus had been arrested and Peter was standing in the courtyard? He tried his best to be "incognito" as he warmed his hands by the fire (Luke 22:55). He just wanted to blend in with the crowd and not be recognized. All Peter had to do was open his mouth and he was in trouble. A young girl recognized him but he quickly denied, "Not me. I don't know him."

The NIV and other translations read, "Sure you were with him. Your speech gives you away." I like the King James reading of the verse: "Thy speech betrayeth thee." I don't know enough about the language to understand, but obviously, there are various dialects and accents in Aramaic, just as there are in the English language.

"Your speech gives you away." Kind of scary, isn't it? My accent is a clear indication that I'm from the South, but are there indicators that I'm a Christian? Does my speech give me away? It's an interesting cycle - Jesus said in Matthew 6:21, "Where your treasure is, there your heart will be also." Later in Matthew 12:34 He says, "For out of the overflow of the heart, the mouth speaks."

That tells me what's in our hearts is what's most important to us. Also, what's in our hearts is eventually going to come out of our mouths. Conclusion: we talk about what's most important to us. We tell our story with our words and our conversations. We pull the curtain back and give a clear view of the window to our hearts when we open our mouths.

Do I find it easy to share what's on my heart? Do I allow Jesus to occupy my heart so much that I can't help but talk about Him and share Him with others? I love the story in Mark 5 of the crazy guy yelling and screaming at the Apostles and Jesus. He was the guy possessed by all those demons and Jesus cast them out of him by sending them into the pigs. After being in his right mind, he begged Jesus to include him in His group. Jesus told him, "No. Go back to your family and tell them what the Lord has done for you."

Rather simple instruction. Just tell what the Lord has done for you. Make him part of your conversation. Make His will so important to you that you can't help but make it obvious every time you open your mouth.

Who are you? Whose are you? What matters most to you?

Just say a few words - it eventually will be very obvious.

MARCH - WEEK ONE

A Nurse Wears Many Hats Psalm 46:1

As I think back over the time I worked in the Emergency Room at Huntsville Hospital, there are some days that stand out vividly in my mind. Most of them were tough days when I saw people die or suffer a tremendous amount of pain. Some were patients. Some were loved ones of patients. Some were hard working doctors, nurses or techs taking care of patients. Watching them hurt, at times took its toll on my heart, but the lessons I learned are certainly immeasurable to my life and that experience made an impact that will last forever with me.

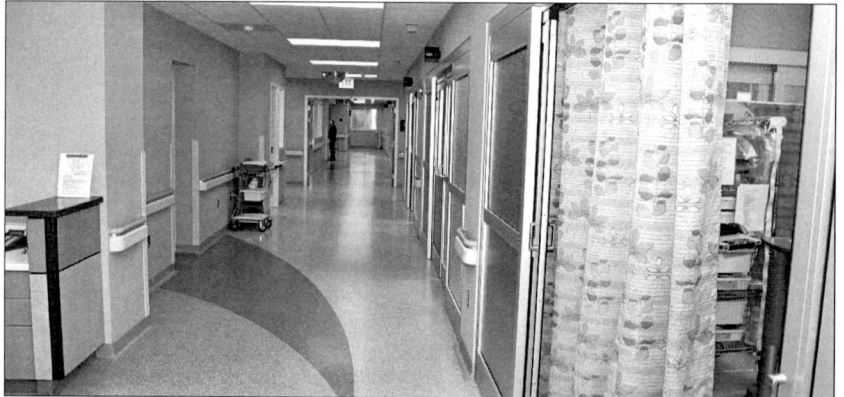

One January morning, everything seemed to be routine...but then again, NOTHING is ever routine in the ER. Not this ER, anyway. It's the busiest ER in the state of Alabama and the only Level 1 trauma hospital in North Alabama. We never knew what was coming but I can guarantee you this - that staff was and is always prepared for anything. The announcement came over the loud speaker:

"LEVEL 1, TRAUMA, D-44, 5 MINUTES"

A few moments later my beeper rang out and the message read:

"LEVEL 1 TRAUMA, D-44, PEDESTRIAN STRUCK- 20 MONTH OLD"

Anytime we got a trauma call, I always got those butterflies in my stomach, but when the patient was a child, those butterflies were more like nails going right through my gut.

"Oh, please, Lord! Not a kid!"

Before I had time to stop and think or allow my emotions to tear up (just thinking of a 20-month old being hit by a car was already getting to me) the nurses and techs rushed to trauma room D-44. They began putting on the trauma gowns, pulling all of the proper equipment in the room, paging radiology and making sure surgery was aware of what was coming, just in case. Nurses from the Pediatric ER rushed over as well as one of the physicians.

Anytime that staff prepared for a trauma, I stood, watched and silently prayed for each one of them - asking God to guide their minds, steady their hands and hold their hearts. "Do we have a child's c-collar ready? Make sure we have the right size needles for IVs. Did HEMSI say if he was intubated?" The charge nurse made sure everything was in place and ready to go. "Make sure everybody is standing right where they're suppose to be. Dr. Najjar wants it quiet and organized."

The staff gloved up and stood there anxiously waiting for the patient. "They're here!" I announced to the room as I saw the EMTs rush down the hall pushing the gurney. The screams of a child's terror rang out as they rolled him into D-44. The Paramedic reported, "Twenty month old male, struck on the right side as a vehicle backed out of a drive-way. Unknown GCS. No LOC. BP is 110 over 70. SAT is 96. Positive deformity in right femur ..." He continued on as I had the heartbreaking task of stopping that child's mother from going in the room. Not allowing a Mother to be by the side of her injured, screaming child was not my favorite duty, but you do what you HAVE to do. I put my arm around her and directed her to the waiting room just a few doors away from her child.

"They'll let you be with him in a few minutes. We just need to get some information."

Through her tears she was able to tell me of any allergies her son had, his past medical history and any other information that will help the staff. Her tears flowed but she wasn't hysterical. She was able to tell me exactly what happened and what caused the accident.

"My brother was in his car getting ready to leave and we were talking. He was standing right there beside me. The next thing I know my brother pulls out and that's when I see Tim behind the car. The car hit him - I screamed and he stopped without running completely over him."

I went back to the trauma room to pass along the Mother's information to the staff. As I relayed the information to the Primary Nurse and physician it was so difficult for them to even hear because of the screams from this little guy. "His lungs are definitely OK!" The physician was checking every inch of him as ultra sound and x-ray did their jobs. The injured child continued to scream and was terrified as these strangers were gathered all around him. Some were poking him with needles. Some were pulling on his arms and legs. Some were putting cold jelly on his belly for the ultra sound. All indications were that this little fellow was going to be OK but we had to make sure.

"How's he ever going to settle down and be still enough for a CT Scan?" My question was unanswered because everybody knew there was no way this little fellow was going to be calm enough for a clear scan. It was then one of those amazing trauma nurses stepped behind the baby and placed her hands on his trembling shoulders. *(continued)*

A Nurse Wears Many Hats (cont.)

(cont.) Cindy Cooper is an experienced, educated Registered Nurse. Her knowledge is superior, and her ability to communicate with her patients is far better than most. I had seen her work her magic on the roughest of irrate patients, drunks, drug seekers, psych patients and any of the others treated by her. Now, there she was with a helpless baby boy screaming at the top of his lungs. I breathed a sigh of relief as I thought to myself, "Timmy - you're in good hands. Yeah, she's a phenomenal nurse. But, she's an even better Mommy." She has 2 of her own.

Cindy calmly and sweetly spoke to the boy, "Hey Timmy. It's OK, Buddy. You're OK. We're going to let Mommy back here in just a few minutes." He continued to scream and squirmed best he could. Cindy continued to ease his fears. Being the "wimp" of the group, I had to step out of the room. My composure was going out the window and I had to take a minute to suck it up. I hated for family members to see me cry so I had to just go take a few deep breaths before I reported an update to that Mother.

Within a few minutes, the screams stopped. The little fellow was lying there calmly. I walked to the Primary Nurse almost in a panic, "Is he OK? Why is he not crying?"

Josiah, one of the techs, had a big grin on his face and pointed at the patient with Cindy standing at the head of the gurney. Cindy was softly rubbing the top of his head and in her calm soothing voice she simply sang to him, *"Jesus loves me this I know, for the Bible tells me so..."*

The room was silent and much less chaotic. The little fellow's breathing was normal and a small crooked smile came across his face. They were able to get him down the hall for the CT Scan and finished the remainder of his treatment. Walking out of CT, I saw the nurses stand beside his gurney, but it was Cindy holding the little guy's hand and continuing to sing, *"Yes, Jesus loves me. Yes, Jesus loves me. Yes, Jesus loves me.*

Our lives can be much like a busy Emergency Room- one crisis right after the other. Without any warning it hits and it hurts and it makes you ask a lot of questions. Things become chaotic. We get scared and we feel all alone. This happened to Jesus's apostles. We read in Luke 8:22 that Jesus and his apostles were in a boat. A squall came down the lake and the boat was tossed about, terrifying the apostles. I'm told that a squall is the most horrific of storms - comparable to a hurricane. Jesus was at the bottom of the boat sound asleep. The apostles awoke Him and begged Him to save their lives. He rebuked the wind and raging waters with a simple command. Once again, calmness was restored over the sea.

When I read those verses I don't feel that Jesus is reprimanding His apostles when He asked them, "Where is your faith?" At least they knew who to run to when they were scared. Do we know who to run to? Do we know who is the One who can truly calm the storms of our lives.

He can still calm the storms in our lives. No matter how often they come. No matter how strong they are. He can still simply command, "Peace Be Still" and calmness prevails. Watching Cindy softly caress that little boy's head and tenderly sing that old precious song, I was reminded of the fact that when we invite Jesus into our crisis, we invite peace - all you have to do is ask Him.

Brandon, Cindy, and Nancy - trauma specialists on the front line in Huntsville's ER.

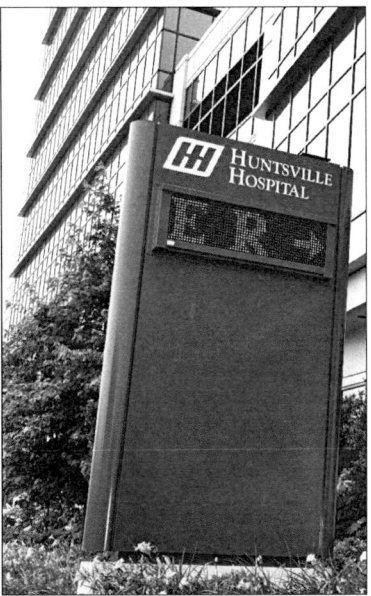

Huntsville Hospital Emergency Room - the busiest trauma unit in Alabama

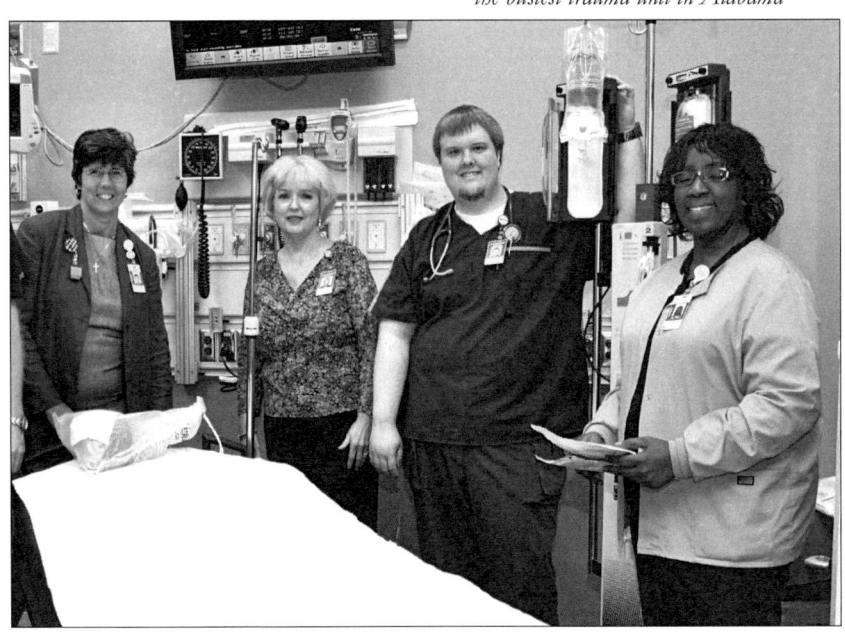

Me, Penny, Will and Dorothy in Trauma Room D-44

25

MARCH - WEEK TWO

A Lesson From Jimmy Buffett? Matt. 19:13-14

My friend, Sisty and I have a private joke that we share every now and then. We'll be shopping or eating somewhere and we'll see a child just wandering around and oblivious to his/her surroundings. Children are so easily distracted and the silliest of things can hold their attention. Perhaps they're walking through the mall or following a parent in a store when a blinking light or something random just catches their eye and they have no clue which direction they're going nor do they have any worry in the world.

Sisty and I will sometimes see a child like this, look at each other and say, *"Tire Swing."*

We call that a "Tire Swing Kid." We base that title on a song written and performed by one of my favorite artists, Alabama native, Jimmy Buffett. His song, "Life's Just a Tire Swing" tells a story of growing up as a child and he had no worries, felt no pain and never allowed the world to interfere with his life:

> *"...and I'd never been west of New Orleans or east of Pensacola*
> *The only contact with the outside world was an RCA Victrola*
> *Life's just a tire swing, 'Jambalaya' was the best song we could sing*
> *Blackberry pickin', eatin' fried chicken and I never knew a thing about pain*
> *'Cause life's just a tire swing"*

It's a catchy little tune and I find myself humming it quite often. It's on my iPod and I have it on CD, as I do almost every song Jimmy Buffett recorded. It makes me smile because I see that philosophy so often with children. The world around them is in a big hurry or rushing into crazy chaos and many times a child will just roll with the flow.

Growing up in the 1960s, I had no clue what turmoil our world was in. In 1968, I was six years old. Senator Robert F. Kennedy was assassinated. Martin Luther King was assassinated. College campuses were in riots and the activities in Vietnam were in full force. All I remember from Vietnam was the sound from the TV of helicopters flying and Walter Cronkite reporting, "Today in Saigon..." I knew there were a lot of people worried about their husbands, sons and grandsons over there, but I really had no idea what was going on. To be honest, I didn't want to know. My biggest worry was if my bicycle tire had enough air and if Dad would give me a nickel for a Milky Way candy bar.

26

When do we lose that way of thinking? When do we allow the world to drag us down to the point where all we do is worry? The economy continues to plunge. My 401K is now a 202D or worse. Retirement? Yeah, right. I've got to work five years after I'm dead. Our friends on the east coast experienced an earthquake one week and a hurricane the next. They've got to be thinking, "What's next?"

In Luke 18, we read of parents bringing their children to Jesus so he can touch them and bless them. Evidently, there was something about Jesus that attracted children and made them feel safe and secure. That's why you cannot convince me that our Savior went through His days with a long face, never smiling and constantly speaking in a negative tone. Not the Jesus I know. If we're created in God's image (and we are) then God has a sense of humor. A baby does not have to be taught to laugh. Within a few weeks following birth, if something amuses a child you will hear that first laugh. Eventually, that laugh becomes a cackle or giggle and there are few things cuter than hearing a child when his "giggle box is turned over."

That's how I picture Jesus with these children in Luke 18 - laughing, playing and knowing what it's like to have fun. It's the grown-ups who get their feathers ruffled and try to move the children out of the way. Jesus rebukes them and says, "Let the little children come unto me..." It's in verse 17 He drives home His point. "Unless you accept the kingdom as children, then you cannot enter." Again, Jesus uses these least likely candidates to be His evangelists. Innocent children that have no clue about the worries of the world or any idea what the future holds. It's these little preachers that Jesus presents before us and says, "Be like them."

In other verses, we're told to grow-up and be mature. The writer of Hebrews wrote we shouldn't remain on milk for our sustenance, but rather move on to meat and other substantial sources of nutrition. The basic message throughout the book of James is, "Grow up!" God does intend for us to mature in our Christianity and grow.

Any living thing must grow or it will die. While this may sound like a contradiction, it really blends beautifully. Jesus is not commanding us to be immature but rather, like children be totally dependent on Him. A child doesn't dwell on negative thoughts and worries. A child doesn't mindlessly watch the news every time it's on the air. No doubt, one of the strongest sources of negative thoughts that goes in our minds are these 24 hour news networks. Why can't we as adults take on the same thought process as a child, "Why do I need to know that?" The way these networks can analyze and dissect events...it's just ridiculous.

Being as little children means that, like a child, we give unconditional love. There's no merit system or keeping score. A child forgives and forgets quickly. A child is humble enough to ask questions of who, why, when, where, etc...rather than assuming he/she has all the answers. A child takes time to play and enjoy life rather than neglect family or a friend because the house is dirty, the yard needs mowing or "there's just too much to get done."

Maybe it's time to be a kid again. I'm not saying be like Peter Pan and refuse to grow up and take on necessary responsibility. I'm saying never lose the innocence that we had as children. Turn the news off and switch it over to "The Andy Griffith Show" or "I Love Lucy." Start the day off in the Word of God, not the word of CNN.

So lighten up - life's just a tire swing!

MARCH - WEEK THREE

Cuttin' Down The Nets   *II Timothy 4:7-8*

Walking up and down the halls of Huntsville Hospital, you never know what you're going to see or who you're going to meet. One Monday morning, I stepped in a couple of rooms and spoke to some patients making sure everything was going OK. Then, I walked in that one special room. That room that has the patient that is going to hold my heart for a while.

She was an elderly lady struggling to walk to the sink from her bed. I asked if I could assist her and she simply said, "I just want to brush my teeth." Not being medically trained, I am very limited as to what I can do to assist a patient but helping someone brush their teeth was definitely something I could handle. I immediately noticed the yellow band on her wrist next to her hospital ID band which indicates "fall risk." I let her hold my arm and I supported her as she sat in a chair I had moved next to the sink. It was then I brushed her teeth as gently as I could, not wanting to harm her in anyway.

Once we completed the task, I assisted her back in the bed and made my way to the door. She said, "Hey, wait a minute. A person brushes your teeth for you it would be nice to get to know them a little better." I chuckled as I sat down in the chair and smiled. She asked my name and said, "Now besides brushing people's teeth, what do you do around here?"

It was then that we began a conversation and quickly became friends. At 85 years old she still had an incredibly sharp mind and told me about her life. Her husband had passed away five years ago. She told me with pride about her two sons, one in Montgomery and one in North Carolina. She bragged about her five grandchildren and two great-grandchildren. She went on to tell me that she had cancer years ago, but the doctor was concerned it could be back. What she thought was the "crud" could be much worse.

Every day for the next two and a half weeks, I went by her room. She was such a joy that a couple of days, I'd eat a quick sandwich in the office and spend the rest of my lunch visiting with this special patient. I'd tease her when I walked in the room and tell her, "I hope you know that you've been voted favorite patient of this hospital."

She'd laugh and say, "Well, that's a big honor unless you've only seen one patient besides me." She would begin to tell me about her growing up days in Kentucky and the farm she was raised on. She was a huge basketball fan (as most Kentuckians are) so she made sure her TV was on during the NCAA tournament. I got tickled at her explaining to me how the winning team celebrates the victory of winning a basketball tournament. "The winners cut down the nets. I've got my bracket ready to see who will be cutting them down this year." Not being a basketball fan, I don't get real fired up about brackets and who's going to win the "big dance", but she obviously loved it so I played along.

A few days later I stopped by, she was lying flat on her back. Didn't have much strength and could hardly speak. I hesitated going in her room and I asked the nurse, "Is she OK?" The nurse interpreted her chart for me which indicated that the cancer was fast and she was declining rapidly.

The oxygen mask covered most of her face but her smile shined through like the sun on a cloudy summer day. I patted her hand and asked if she was comfortable. She nodded yes and I sat for a few minutes as she faded off to sleep. The next few days she got weaker and weaker but I continued to stop by just to say hello.

One afternoon, I stepped in for a quick hello. The decline in her condition became quite obvious and I guess the tear in my eye that I tried to hide was obvious. That smile came through again and she asked me:

"Is that a tear or have you got hay fever?"

I didn't reply, I just patted her hand. It was then she took my hand, pulled me right up to her face and whispered:

"We win! We cut down the nets. Jesus made sure of that."

She's right! No matter what is thrown my way and no matter how tough this fight gets - WE WIN! I took a sneak at the last chapter and she's right- WE WIN! We all cut down the nets.

I love the verse in Proverbs 21:31 "The horse is made ready for the day of battle, but victory rests with the Lord." In other words, do all the preparing you want to do- the battle belongs to the Lord.

The next Friday morning I got to my office and began organizing my day. The phone rang and I knew by the caller ID what the news would be. Just as I hung up from the conversation a co-worker stepped in my office. She saw an unusual look on my face and had to ask, "You OK?"

I grinned real big and answered: *"Sure! Kentucky just cut down the nets."*

MARCH - WEEK FOUR

Martha, Martha — Philippians 1:3

There are some people in the Bible who get a "bad rap". They are misunderstood or their actions are taken out of context and they are labeled and categorized, many times unfairly. Thomas has been labeled "Doubting Thomas" because he was skeptical the first time he heard Jesus had risen from the dead. I wouldn't say he doubted, I'd just say he was making extra sure. All it took was for him to see the nail scars in Jesus's hands and he believed immediately. No questions asked and no going back.

The Mother of James and John is categorized as an "opportunist" as she makes a bold request of Jesus recorded in Matthew 20. "Sir, when you establish your kingdom please allow one of MY sons to sit on your left side and the other on your right." I always wanted to cut this poor Mother some slack. Sure, she missed the point of what the kingdom was all about, but at least she had her children's best interest in mind. Seems to me after one explanation from Jesus, she understood and never asked again.

Jesus spent a lot of time in the home of Mary and Martha. They lived in Bethany and obviously they were followers and believers of our Savior. He could get a good meal there and share some words from His Father with others. Luke 10 gives an account of Jesus speaking and Mary hanging on to every word that He's saying.

For years, this scene has been easy to picture in my mind. Of course, the home I envision is more conducive to ours in the western hemisphere. I see Martha in a small kitchen, bringing hot bread out of the oven, stirring some beans on the stove and cutting a steaming pot roast that's ready to be served. In the other room, Jesus is sitting on a comfortable sofa and Mary is in the chair right next to Him, completely mesmerized by every word coming out of His mouth.

I realize that my vision of this scene is quite modern and that's not how things were in the first century. But, I bet my thinking isn't too far off. The point is the same. Martha is focused on tasks and Mary is focused on people. She even whines to Jesus, "Don't you care that I'm doing all of this work and Mary won't help me?" Jesus is very calm in His response to her, "Martha, Martha." I picture him shaking his head and maybe even grinning when He says, "Dear, Sweet, Martha - don't you understand? Mary has chosen what's important."

Martha Kimbrough (right) speaking at the Annual Ladies Conference in Havana, Cuba

I have a dear friend, Martha Kimbrough, and every now and then I like to tease her and refer to her as "Martha, Martha." It's quite a dichotomy for me to refer to her that way. If anyone has conquered the art of balancing their life it's Martha Kimbrough. Many times I've heard Dad make the comment, "I've got to get to the hospital. They've taken 'so and so' to the ER. I'm sure Martha Kimbrough is already there so she can fill me in." If a meal needs to be cooked, a visit to a hospital needs to be made, a note of encouragement needs to be written or a grieving soul needs a hug - Martha Kimbrough is either there or on her way.

I think in Luke 10, the rebuking that Martha received is justified and many of us should be rebuked the same way. Many of us get so caught up in tasks that we lose sight of what really matters and what's most important. Sadly, I have some friends who think back over their childhood and recall, "I have no memories of sitting in my Mother's lap and her reading a book to me, but you can bet that house was clean as a whistle. Rather than taking us on an afternoon picnic or playing with us in the yard, she had us dusting the blinds or scrubbing the sink.

It's too easy for me to be critical of fastidious housekeepers because, well...let's just say I would never win an award for my clean house. I wouldn't say my house is dirty, but clutter does tend to accumulate. Too often I choose to be with people rather than my vacuum cleaner. I'm not ashamed of that and I make no apology for it.

Don't get me wrong. Taking care of our household chores are a must. The Lord never intended for us to ignore our duties at home, whether married or single. It just makes me sad to see those who get so caught up in the things that really don't matter. Ironing and dusty furniture will be there tomorrow. Some people won't be.

Is it possible to be too involved with church activities that we miss the point? ABSOLUTELY! Being involved and being connected is imperative, but many times our focus is on the task itself - not on the purpose. Too often, we lose sight that the church must be about PEOPLE rather than tasks. Granted, helping people involves a task, but it's when we become the perfectionist like Martha in Luke 10 that we fail.

I heard a story once of a post office being built in a major city. This brand new facility had state of the art equipment, the best conveyor belts to move the boxes of mail through, rows and rows of mailboxes for customers and even an area where the most avid stamp collector can come and purchase items. You know what they forgot? The slots where people can mail their letters. You could buy any type of stamp you wanted, but there was no receptacle for you to insert that letter!

What purpose is a post office if you can't mail a letter? What purpose is a church if you can't reach people? If church leadership is focused on tasks rather than hearts, we might as well cut the lights out and sell the building.

Martha, Martha! While it is necessary that a meal is prepared, what an opportunity she missed to sit and listen directly to the words of Jesus.

Cindi, Cindi! What opportunities are you and I missing?

In this world of "I'm so busy" being a status symbol and a button of prestige, am I cheating myself of the precious, valuable gift of time - time with a friend, time with my family and better yet, time with the Savior? I pray one day I learn to balance it all.

MARCH - WEEK FIVE

I Want To See Jesus — *Revelation 21:3*

The Bible makes reference to all five of our senses. In Matthew 13:16, Jesus is explaining why he taught in parables when he said, " But blessed are your eyes because they see and your ears because they hear." In Mark 5:28 we read of a woman who was suffering from an issue of blood and says, "If I can just touch His clothes, I know I will be healed."

In Matthew 13, Jesus tells many parables to his disciples regarding the Kingdom of Heaven. He shares a story of seeds being planted and falling on four different types of ground. The seed represents the word of God and the soil is the heart of the listeners and how receptive we are. Another is a parable of the sower who planted seed with wheat and weeds. After that one, He compares the kingdom to a mustard seed that is planted and is very tiny, but grows into a tall, strong tree. After each parable, Jesus challenges His disciples by saying, "He who has ears to hear, let him hear."

In Matthew 26, we read of Jesus instituting the Lord's Supper with His apostles and teaching us all the example of tasting the bread which represents His body and drinking the cup which represents His blood.

One of my topics for ladies retreats is entitled "The Aroma of Christ" and I share Paul's statement in II Corinthians 2:14-15 which reads, "...and through us spreads everywhere the fragrance of the knowledge of him. For we are to God the aroma of Christ." I try to challenge those good ladies to make sure their Christian lives are like a sweet aroma and this fragrance is shared to outsiders and others who are hurting.

Seeing, hearing, tasting, touching, smelling...all five of them right there in my Bible. As I think about the five senses, I ask myself which one would be the most painful to lose. I'm thankful I have all 5 but which one can I not do without. My friend, Jason Bybee does not have a sense of smell and I can't imagine how difficult that would be. I'm sure it came in handy for him when he changed diapers for his three children.

Without hesitation, I'd have to say I would hate to lose the gift of sight. The ability to see is truly something I hope I never take for granted and how I pity anyone who has completely lost their sight.

From March through May of 2009, I'm not sure when I've been more thankful for the gift of sight. I saw many things for the very first time and they made a tremendous impact on me. They're things I will never forget for the rest of my life.

The last weekend of March my dear friend Karen Brunner and I spent a few days in New York City and covered a tremendous amount of territory in a short period of time, thanks to her outstanding tour guide skills. The Statue of Liberty, The Empire State Building, St. Patrick's Cathedral, Ground Zero, Times Square, Ellis Island, Rockefeller Plaza, all of these landmarks that I've only seen on television or in the movies were right before my eyes.

I wrote these thoughts while sitting in the Los Angeles airport enduring a four hour layover on my way home. My mind was replaying a mental video of what I saw on the Saturday of my weekend in Fresno, California. My hostess, and new friend in Fresno,

Kelley Young took me to Yosemite National Park that afternoon and we saw the falls as well as the The Sequoias. Kelley had only known me less than 24 hours so she had no idea how rare it is for me to be speechless, but I was. Talking on the phone with Dad, I shared with him the experience of seeing Yosemite for the first time and all he could do is laugh because I was so hyper and just out of breath as I searched for words to describe it to him. All I could think about was Paul's writing in Romans 1: 19-20 that God is seen plainly in nature.

So many of these sights I had seen on television or in a book, but it did not do them justice. I saw the tallest mountain of granite in the world for the first time. The falls including the "Bridal Veil" were breath taking. I saw trees that stand over 300 feet in the air with trunks as wide as some houses. I saw the snow capped Rocky Mountains from 32,000 feet in the air and the Sierra Mountains as I flew from Denver to Los Angeles.

My eyes were scanning as I watched people walk by in the Los Angeles airport and I kept thinking maybe a big celebrity would walk by. How much fun would it be to see some big movie star or singer or movie producer.

That prompted me to think of some famous people I had met. I got to meet and shake hands with Paul "Bear" Bryant one time. I remember when I was about 10 years old Governor George C. Wallace invited me to the Governors Mansion in Montgomery and I got to meet him, shake his hand and have him sign a photo for me. During visits to Nashville, Tennessee, I've spotted a few country music stars. I saw Faith Hill pumping her own gasoline one time. Dad and I saw Kenny Rogers in a restaurant in Nashville once and another time in the airport I saw Lee Greenwood. No doubt, the most famous person I've ever met is former first lady, Barbara Bush. She was a gracious lady as she hugged my neck and said, "Please give this hug to all in the great state of Alabama."

Seeing famous people and attractions in this country for the first time is exciting and it leaves mental images in my mind that last a lifetime. All of the amazing sights and amazing people that I might see in this lifetime can NEVER compare to the fact that one day I will actually stand face to face with my Lord and Savior Jesus Christ. Oh... the thought of that just gives me chills. Not only will I get to stand off at a distance and just catch a glimpse of Him, I'll get to see him face to face. I'll get to see heaven and the home prepared for me. I'll get to see those people that I love who have been in heaven for a while. I missed them on this earth so much - Wo, Granddaddy Ed, Mom and Pop Strickland, Melisa's sweet Daddy, Jack Miller, Marsha Glenn, well...that list could go on and on.

There is so much I want to see on this beautiful earth of ours. Even right here in our own great country, there are so many other sights I want to see and people I would love to meet. But, when I think of the promise He has made and the promise of one day seeing Him face to face, I hear the voice of God tell me, "Cindi, you ain't seen nothin' yet."

"And the righteous will see His holy face - washed in the blood, saved by His grace
To the righteous He promises this special place - right next to His heart face to face"

APRIL - WEEK ONE

But, I'm A Doctor *Matthew 18:4*

"How long is the wait for a table?" The other patrons of the restaurant were seated in the lobby, standing at the door and waiting outside on the benches. Friday nights are always busy for local eateries and at 7:00 pm it was quite a rush. The young hostess looked through her long list and responded, "Sir, right now it's at least an hour wait. I'll be glad to take your name." "Smith. DOCTOR Smith." He put quite an emphasis when he said "DOCTOR" and leaned toward her as he said it. I had to chuckle as I watched the hostess write down his name. The way the DOCTOR emphasized his name it was as if she was supposed to go wash her hands and get a fresh pen prior to adding him to the list.

At least four times prior to being seated he went to the hostess desk and asked once again, "How long for DOCTOR Smith." The response was the same. The hostess would call out another name and that would prompt him to again step up and ask, "How long?"

I felt sympathy for that hostess as she was multi-tasking and trying to maintain that sweet smile on her face. It was obvious there were no available tables and continuing to ask someone who had absolutely no control over the situation was not going to speed up the process. Most of the patrons were patient but a few, including the DOCTOR, paced and quite often leaned over the hostess desk and viewed the list.

Working in a comparable occupation as that hostess, my heart went out to her. In the surgical waiting room of an 880 bed hospital, there are those who tend to be impatient and feel there is no need that THEY should wait. It's always interesting at a hospital where there are rules and regulations that are perceived as unnecessary. Too easily, we forget that the purpose of a hospital is to care for the patient - not the visitor. That's not to say that the visitor is not important and crucial to the patient's healing process.

Patients have quite an ordeal before going to the operating room. For one thing, they are dressing and that requires privacy. The nurse is starting an IV and asking private medical questions. The anesthesiologist steps in and a few moments later the surgeon comes in to check the patient. A small room is not conducive for many visitors so we require that only one family member be with the patient until a few moments prior to surgery. At that point, the nurse gives me the go ahead to allow others to see the patient, have prayer and give their well wishes.

In a conversation with Dad, I asked him, *"Would you like to guess who the rudest visitors are to my waiting room?"* He knew it was a loaded question and sarcastically he responded, "OH! Preachers, I'm sure."

"RIGHT!" We laughed and I told him it's so frustrating, because they think that I don't understand how crucial prayer is before a surgery. If anybody understands that, it's me.

One morning a man dressed nicely bypassed my desk and walked through the double doors to the pre-op area. I jumped up calling, *"Sir, Sir?"* He stopped and looked at me.

Before I could utter a word he snapped, *"I'm Father David* (not his real name). *The patient in room 8 phoned me and asked me to come pray with her."* He turned abruptly and continued his way past the nurse's station.

To my surprise, a doctor stopped the man and kindly said, *"Sir, this lady is trying to tell you something. You'll need to step back to the waiting room."* I explained that I needed to check with the nurse and make sure it is an appropriate time. It was so disappointing because a vast majority of the priests, ministers, rabbis, pastors and other members of the clergy that come to our hospital are kind, cooperative and compliant with our polices. They understand that a patient's medical information MUST remain private and they understand that complying with that is not only hospital policy, but also a federal law.

When this man found a seat in the waiting room, I kindly pointed to the coffee pot and offered for him to help himself. *"That's a fresh pot - and you'll find cups, sweeteners and creamer right there on the stand."*

He stepped over, poured a cup of coffee and asked, *"Why don't you have any Equal?"* I apologized and offered him the stuff in the pink packet. While stirring his sweetener he, in all seriousness, asked, *"Do you have a sweet roll or something to go with this coffee?"*

I honestly thought he was teasing but by the look on his face and tone in his voice, he was as serious as a confession. Far too many times, thoughts go through my head and far too many times people make it difficult for me to keep them from falling from my lips.

My thought was, "DUDE! Do you see a 'Dinner on the Ground' sign anywhere?" I kept my thoughts to myself and invited him to visit our cafeteria where they serve a full breakfast until 10:00 every morning.

"It doesn't apply to me." Is that the mentality we take on sometimes? A sense of entitlement seems to be building in our society and I just can't seem to pinpoint the source of it. Maybe we feed it in people when we show favoritism like we read about in James 2. He writes (I'm paraphrasing) that if someone dressed in fine clothes and favorable appearance comes in your assembly, don't fall all over yourself to accommodate them and make sure they have the best seat in the house, while everybody else fends for themselves.

On the same line, others feel they don't have to work for a living because the government will take care of them and provide for their needs. After all, each American citizen is entitled to that. Right? Nowhere in the Bible do I read that a title by our name entitles us.

Sadly, how we act in public brings disrespect to that title, especially if it is in conjunction with the work of God. Jesus taught that if we humble ourselves then we will be lifted up (James 4:10). Have you noticed that anytime He commands for us to follow Him, the first step is to humble yourself? Many of the interpretations of the parables is that the last shall be first.

Back to the restaurant, the hostess called out over the speaker, "DR. SMITH, YOUR TABLE IS NOW AVAILABLE, DR. SMITH!" He approached the hostess and she continued, *"Sir, we can seat you and your wife now."*

His response? *"She's not my wife."*

His date's response: *"He's not a doctor."*

APRIL - WEEK TWO

He Picks Me Every Time   John 3:16

Every high school junior or senior approaches prom season with great anticipation. Back in my day, instead of a prom, we had a banquet. Somewhere in that mysterious second chapter of Jude, it reads that it's wrong to dance. So, we had a nice dinner at a fancy location. The memory of preparing for that banquet is clear, but the highest priority was who would be my date.

His name was Todd. OK - that's not his real name but let's protect the innocent here. I had a HUGE crush on Todd! He was perfect. I honestly think when I saw him, I could hear Karen Carpenter sing:

"Why do birds suddenly appear, everytime you are near..."

Every girl in school thought the same about Todd.

Todd was in Philip's class, a year ahead of me and we were in the same study hall. Why did they call it STUDY HALL? There was no studying and we weren't in a hall.

The first week of school, I settled in a desk as others filed in and to my surprise who sat down in front of me but Todd. I almost fainted when he actually turned around and said, "Hey Bradley. What's up?" It was as if the air would not come up from my lungs and my vocal cords would not constrict. I just gave a nervous grin. Why in the world would this boy sit next to me and be nice to me? Did he lose a bet? Was this a joke? As the weeks went on, I'd still get those silly butterflies in study hall, but eventually, my conversations with Todd relaxed. He actually thought I was funny. Not as funny as Philip, but who is?

Todd had a girlfriend that went to another school and that, along with being so far out of my league, negated any possibility of him asking me out. Of course, he had a girlfriend and she was gorgeous with perfect hair, perfect teeth, a perfect complexion and a perfect life. She probably spent her time reading to the blind or feeding the poor.

Then it happened. We returned from Spring Break, and I saw Todd moping around from class to class. He walked in study hall with his head down and looking like someone had just stolen his lunch money. I curiously asked, *"How's it going?"*

"She dumped me, Bradley. She actually dumped me. The girl of my dreams broke up with me."

I've never heard The Mormon Tabernacle Choir perform live, but the way they sounded in my head belting out "The Hallelujah Chorus" was in high definition. Could it actually be? Could this be my chance to finally turn this friendship into something MUCH more? Could that wedding I had planned in my head for Todd and me come true? Yeah, I already had names for our children.

"You were too good for her, Todd. You deserve better." Oh, the build up had started and I was laying it on thick. From that time on, I became his counselor, advisor,

confidant and emotional pit stop. Anytime he asked if he should call her, I was quick to respond, *"NO! Let her go!"*

I was feeling pretty confident as the Junior-Senior Banquet was approaching. I was the only girl Todd talked to for a few weeks and my hopes, dreams and prayers were that I'd be his date. I already had the pretty light blue dress bought and it would match perfectly with the light blue tuxedo he would wear, (remember, this was 1978).

A week or so passed and then finally, he approached the topic. He turned around in his desk and with his perfect blonde feathered bangs dipping over one eye he asked, *"Hey Bradley, you going to the banquet?"* I almost hyperventilated. Here was my chance.

OK, Cindi. Don't blow it. Take a deep breath and don't be too eager. *"Sure, I'm going. Just don't know with whom."* I was hoping he'd get the hint. Could it be that he would pick me? Could he actually want ME to be his date - to be the one that would be picked up in his brand new Chevy Camaro. Would I be the one walking in that banquet with the cutest boy at school? ME?

"I've been thinking a lot about who to ask." His brown eyes looked down as he talked. *"Since the break-up, I haven't been interested in any other girl but I know I can't go by myself. I wanted to ask you because I really trust you."* I braced myself as he continued,

"Cindi, do you think Becky would go with me?"

My face fell. I tried not to let my eyes tear up because my heart was broken. *"Todd, I'm sure she'll go with you. She'd be crazy not to. She's pretty and popular so you better ask her soon before someone else does."*

My world was crushed. All I could do was sit in my room and listen to my Barry Manillow albums and wish things were different. Why didn't he pick me? Why wasn't I the one chosen?

Not being picked brings about a lot of pain. As we grow older, the times we're not selected are much deeper than a date. For many, that job or promotion is needed so badly and they decided "to go another way." Many college applicants have plans set until they receive that letter saying, "Sorry. You weren't chosen." There are loving wives who are rejected because their husband picked someone else.

Here's the good news - God ALWAYS picks you.

If you were the only person on this earth that needed a savior, Jesus still would have died. Paul tells us in Romans 5:6 that while we were sinners, Jesus died.

Life disappoints, but God never does. He will never lead you on, get your hopes up only to let you down. You can always stand on His promises.

Todd went to the banquet with Becky and I went with another boy. Graduation came, Todd went off to college, got a job, got married and is living out west. Word has it that he turned 50, he's fat, bald and has ugly kids.

God is good.

APRIL - WEEK THREE

First, You've Got To Die — Romans 6

Each spring, I look forward to our family gathering on Easter Sunday. Mother always makes every holiday so special and unique. The trouble she goes to is incredible and she's made it very easy for holidays to be warm, special memories. I think Easter is one of Mother's favorites. She loves spring flowers, bunnies, jelly beans and all that is associated with Easter. Candy jars are filled and placed throughout the house and chocolates are in ample supply.

Most of the time at Easter, we're blessed in Alabama with warm weather and beautiful blooms of spring. I love the dogwoods, Bradford Pears and everything finally turning green after a long cold winter.

Easter 2006 was one of our best. The day came in mid-April so we were seeing warmer temperatures. My cousin Stuart, his wife Brenda and their son, Barrett were visiting from Montgomery. Philip and his family were with us and as usual, Mother put on a spread that was fit for royalty. After a meal like that, it's only natural to want to sit on the porch and let your meal settle.

Sitting out there feeling the warm breezes, Philip and I began to remember Easters from the past. Of course, anytime we remember a time in our childhood, laughter is involved. Easter was crucial in our family because that's when we got our best clothes. Our winter clothes came at Christmas and spring clothes came at Easter.

I told Philip that certain smells quickly come to mind when I remember Easter and he agreed. He said, "Remember how Mom would boil three dozen eggs to dye and then she'd have to boil vinegar to dip them in?" We started laughing because we could picture all of us in the kitchen standing around Mom and watching her dip the eggs in all the different colors.

I added, "Yeah, you take that smell of eggs boiling and the vinegar then throw in the fabulous smell of a Lilt home perm - WHEW!! Not sure which was worse, the eggs or the perm." Mom always insisted on a new perm for my hair. For old times sake, I almost slept in those cute little pink sponge curlers and on Easter morning wore white ankle socks with black patent leather shoes! The worst was that stand-out slip and how it itched my legs. I bet every female remembers those. Along with the memory of those smells, Philip threw in the memory of smelling shoe polish and Brylcream... *"a little dab'll do 'ya".*

I can remember waking up on Easter Sunday morning so excited because the Easter bunny had found our house. My Easter basket was always the best - filled with eggs, chocolate bunnies, Cadbury eggs, chocolate eggs, plastic eggs filled with chocolate, chocolate malt balls, chocolate candy called "Robin Eggs", and some more chocolate. Obviously, the Easter bunny knew I loved chocolate. Even though I was strongly advised not to, I had to dive right in and have a few samples from my Easter basket before getting ready for church. It didn't take long for me to realize that an abundance of chocolate before 7:00 am is not a good idea. There were a few Sundays I sat through church singing, "Up From The Grave He Arose" with a queasy stomach.

Yes, Easter meant new clothes, new shoes, new hair-dos - new everything. Even as adults, we still get new clothes and Dad always gets his new Easter tie. Mom likes to pull out a new Easter dress - and it's on that Sunday we all have permission to break out the white shoes.

Not only are the clothes new at Easter, but the beauty of our world is new. Each year at Easter is usually when the trees are getting greener and greener and the colors around me are becoming more and more vibrant. The azaleas in my front yard are almost breath-taking, as are the dogwood trees and my neighbor's flower beds. All of this came to be because a few months ago they died. They live because they died.

Back in the fall, we watched the beautiful process of death. The trees changing colors and grabbing our undivided attention is actually the process of death. Living so close to the Smoky Mountains, travelers will flock from all over just to see the beautiful trees and the mountains. In all truth, we're looking at death.

It is the same for us as children of God. In order for us to live as Christians, we must first die. Jesus taught this in John 12:23-26. "…unless a kernel of wheat falls to the ground and dies, it remains only a single seed. But, if it dies, it produces many seeds. The man who loves his life will lose it, while the man who hates his life in this world will keep it for eternal life." Like the seed, we must die in order to live.

Paul wrote in I Corinthians 15:36 that if you sow a seed it doesn't live unless it first dies. What a paradox! Jesus taught if you want to be great, you must serve. If you want to be first you must be last. If you want to live, you must die. *So what is he talking about? How can I LIVE for Him if I must DIE first?*

Not a physical death - a spiritual death. Die to the old way of life. Die to my prideful way of thinking. Die to always wanting my way. Die to always thinking of myself first. Die to ME and LIVE for Him. It's not about me. It's about Him. He lives so now I can live for Him - and that's what Easter is all about.

APRIL - WEEK FOUR

After The Storm   *Psalm 46:2-3*

Driving down Paul Bryant Drive in Tuscaloosa, Alabama, I made the left turn on to Hackberry Lane. It was a quiet Sunday morning and I had just said "good-bye" to my dear friends, Kelley and Judy Riley after worshiping with them at University Church of Christ. It was my first time to see the Rileys since the tornadoes hit back in April. The night before in their home, they shared with me their experience of surviving the tornadoes that tore through our state and their hometown of Tuscaloosa.

I told them how I had been in Tuscaloosa two months after the storm and was in shock at the damage on 15th Street. "It's amazing how the layout of that area has changed completely. I almost missed turning on to McFarland Boulevard because the Chevron Station, Krispy Kreme and Full Moon Bar-B-Que were gone."

"Oh, you need to drive down Hackberry and Hargrove Road and other neighborhoods over there." Kelley and Judy concurred that it was a horrible day, but could have been much more horrible had that monster moved 1/4 of a mile north and travelled down University Drive.

"If it had hit that campus, the death toll would have easily been in the hundreds, maybe thousands." Kelley Riley has a heart as soft as a child's and his compassion oozed as he recalled the events of that day.

Taking Kelley's advice, I drove down Hackberry and thankfully, there was little or no traffic behind me, so I could slow down and see it all. I remembered speaking to a group of ladies there at the Central Church of Christ a few years ago. Unbelievable - the building that once seated 600 or more people was now a concrete slab.

My hand went over my mouth as I sat there in that area and tears filled my eyes. I knew what I was seeing in no way came close to what it was like on April 28th, the day after it all hit. I drove through the neighborhood where my friend, Renee Graham's daughters had lived when they were in school at the university. The house was still standing but within 100 yards, all I saw were foundations and clear fields. Not far from there was the field where one of Alabama's football players landed after the tornado literally sucked him out of his house and threw him over 200 yards away. His girlfriend whom he was trying to protect was killed.

From there I pulled in the parking lot of University Mall. Before April 27th, the view to the campus was obstructed by trees and houses, but that morning I could clearly see Coleman Coliseum and all of the buildings of Druid City Hospital. It continued to run through my mind, "Cindi, this is NOTHING compared to how it was. A lot, if not most has been cleaned up."

A security officer with the mall pulled up beside me and asked if I needed help. I told him I was just being a tourist and following the tornado path. He was very kind and said he just wanted to make sure I wasn't lost or need any assistance. "I'm just in awe of all of this and amazed at how quickly something like this can happen."

"Yes, Ma'am. It was quite a day. Have you driven through Alberta City and seen that neighborhood? Those folks took quite a hit, too." I had driven through that area a few months prior to this visit with Melisa and her husband, Barry. He was right. Houses were destroyed and even months afterward, tarps covered the roofs and debris and rubble covered some yards.

Tuscaloosa was just one of many areas in the state that were affected that day. Early that morning Guntersville was hit. Phil Campbell was slammed. The small town of Hackelburg was practically wiped out by an F-5 tornado as well as Pratt City, Cordova, Cullman, Harvest and areas in north Birmingham. Approximately 50 were killed in DeKalb County near Ft. Payne. Areas in Mississippi were hit and my former hometown, Ringgold, Georgia was slammed with a tremendous amount of damage.

I spent that April 27th day with my good friend, Laura Pendergrass, and she's not a native of Alabama. I told her days like that make you aware of some of the great names of small towns in Alabama: Reform (pronounced RE-form), Gordo, Slap Out, Wedowe and my favorite, Chigger Hill. Funny names of towns made up of hard working, salt of the earth-type people that I proudly call my fellow Alabamians.

Five months later, the storms were over. The roar was silenced and the debris was no longer flying in the air. The rain stopped and the wind had died. I asked the security officer, "How do you function after a day like that?"

"Well, you cry a lot. Some of us still cry when we see the destruction. It gets cloudy and there might be a clap of thunder or strong wind and my scared kids come running to me or their Mama." He seemed to have some pride as he continued to speak, "But, you know what? I've never been more proud to be from the state of Alabama in all my life. We may have some good football teams in this state that win championships but, watching everybody pull together, help their fellow man and show the love that we've seen makes you thankful and proud."

He pulled his cap back and continued his thought, "Ma'am, a day like that day, you never get over, but you move on. You bury your dead. You cry. You grieve. You rebuild. You cry again. You move on and pray it never happens again. We could roll around in self-pity and blame everybody from the government to God that something like this happened, but, that doesn't accomplishment a thing. You pick yourself up, brush off the dirt and move on."

David was the King of Israel and he found himself in a storm. Unlike tornado victims, his storm was a consequence of his sin, but, nonetheless, he hurt and cried out to God. He sinned with Bathsheba who later became his wife. She had given birth to the child they had conceived and David was on his knees begging God to spare the child. He didn't eat or sleep or talk to anyone - he just begged God.

In II Samuel 12: 22 David was asked why he was now able to eat and sleep and he answered, "While the child was alive, I fasted and wept but now the child has died. I can't bring him back. So, I go on with life."

Did David just "get over it?" Absolutely not. I don't think he ever just "got over it" but, he adjusted, accepted it and moved on. Maybe easier said than done but, by the grace of God, that's what he did.

Over 250 Alabamians died on April 27, 2011. Businesses were destroyed and lives were changed forever. But, you won't find self-pity or blame. You'll just find hard working people who love their state - pulling together and moving on.

I hope I can do the same when I face a storm.

MAY - WEEK ONE

Stain That Reminds Me Of Pain   I Peter 1:6

I've had the shirt for years and I still wear it occasionally. The stain on the right shoulder has become less and less noticeable but sometimes I can still see it. Any other shirt, I would have thrown out with a stain like that, but not this shirt. It's a favorite and it also holds a special memory to me.

It's a white, long sleeve button down collared shirt with an embroidered University of Alabama emblem on the left side. I bought it many years ago and it has endured wear and tear over a long period of time. That shirt has been everywhere from Bryant-Denny Stadium to casual days at work. I don't remember why I was wearing it on this particular Thursday when the stain occurred, but I had it on with a pair of jeans. I was living in Chattanooga at the time and had been home from work for a few hours. My friend Sisty's son, Taylor, was mowing my grass. The weather had warmed up on this afternoon in May and spring was in full bloom.

My phone rang and my Mother's distressed voice was on the other line. "Cindi, Clay has had a wreck and he's in bad shape. Your Dad and I are on our way to UAB Hospital." My nephew, Clay had turned 16 the previous November and had his drivers license. Driving home from school that afternoon he had been involved in an accident and was flown to UAB hospital.

My heart sank. I never had children of my own but my nephews and nieces are the closest feeling to motherhood I'll ever have. I love them like my own. I knew he was OK but there was no way my mind would ease until I eyeballed him myself. I immediately phoned Sisty and told her I was leaving for Birmingham but, like a true best friend she responded, "No, you're not. Barry and I are on our way. We'll drive you."

I don't remember much about the drive down there, I just remember Barry ignoring the speed limit signs and getting me there as quickly as his Toyota would go. Phone calls along the way brought reports of Clay's status and other details of the accident. Barry grew up in Birmingham so he knew exactly where he was going as we approached the downtown medical district.

The waiting room in the Emergency Department was full but many of them were familiar faces as family and friends gathered. My parents met me at the door and informed me Clay was conscious, doing well, but had many cuts all over his face. Dad instructed me to step over to the desk and let them know I'm here.

"Clay Bradley. I'm his aunt, Cindi Bradley from Chat..." She didn't let me finish.

"Yes. Your brother is back here and asked us to bring you back when you arrived."

Gary met me in the hall as I looked for Clay's room. "He's OK but get ready to see a lot of blood on his face. The doctor said it'll take about 200 stitches."

I stepped in the room and there he was. Lying there, he once again looked three years old, even though he was half grown. I stepped to the side of the bed, leaned down and hugged him like I had not seen him in years. I stayed by his bed while the nurse continued to work. In fact, I was practically lying on the gurney beside him and he rested his head on my shoulder.

42

When he and his brothers were kids, I was the aunt that could rarely say no to them. If they wanted a dollar, I gave them one. If they wanted to eat some place special after a ball game, we ate where they said. One morning, Clay had Doritos and a strawberry Yoohoo for breakfast. No objection from me. Standing in line at the grocery store, if one of them wanted a candy bar, who was I to say no? No was just a word that I rarely used with those guys.

That's what made it difficult watching that doctor put those stitches in Clay's face. He had quickly grown weary of having to lie so still. What he really hated was the pain from the needle and the shots that supposedly deadened the pain. The doctor moved to the side of his face and had to once again put the needle in his cheek. Clay moved his head closer to my shoulder and that's when the blood stained my shirt. He looked at me and whispered, "Make him stop!"

I tried to reason with him and explain that he needed to take more stitches so his face will heal and he won't scar. "Clay, they've got to do this. It's the only way you can get well."

The more I tried to reason the more he begged. "I don't care if I have scars. Please tell him to stop." His begging continued but my "no" had to remain persistent.

That was one of the toughest "NOs" I've ever had to say. My head kept telling me to let that doctor keep working and take as many stitches as he needed to, no matter how painful it was for Clay. My heart spoke much louder telling me to grab that doctor's arm and tell him, "OK - that's enough!" Watching Clay hurt and beg was about all I could stand. I know those needles going in his face hurt awfully bad but, watching him hurt was like a knife right through my heart. All I knew to do was hold him and assure him it was going to be OK.

Any of you who are our parents, no doubt have been in similar situations. You so badly want to take away any pain your children might encounter, whether physical or emotional. But taking away that pain prevents the child from receiving what's best for him/her. I remember when my brother, Philip, and his wife, Kim took their son, Benjamin to get his vaccinations. He was a tiny baby and had not been home from the hospital long.

I phoned Philip when they returned from the pediatrician and I asked him, "Did Ben cry?"

Philip's answer, "Well, no, he didn't cry, but me on the other hand..."

Seeing your child hurt is not an easy thing to see. I'm convinced that God feels the same way when he sees His children hurt. It hurts Him and yes, He has that option to say, "OK - I won't let you go through this." But instead, He chooses to allow pain because if we can't feel pain how can we ever feel joy? He sees each tear, He hears us cry and sometimes, just like any other parent, all He can do is just hold us.

I'll hang on to that shirt a long time because it reminds me that my Heavenly Father has to say:

"No! I know it hurts, but I'm right here."

I Want My Mommy — Proverbs 31

While sitting in a chair on the 18th floor balcony looking out over the Gulf of Mexico, I relaxed as the waves were singing a mellow song and the breeze disheveled my hair. Normally, I don't like for my hair to be messed up but since the breeze was coming from the Gulf, I didn't care. It felt wonderful. Two friends from work and I escaped to Destin, FL for a few days of sun, sand, seafood, laughs and basically to unwind. Except for some clouds one morning the weather had been perfect for Alesa, Judy and me.

It's easy for me to pack up, load my car and run down to the beach when my work schedule allows. I don't need anyone's permission and I don't have to consider anyone else in my house because, I'm the only resident. It has caught my attention how it's never that easy for a Mother. Judy's kids are grown, but Alesa left a 2 ½ year old and an 11-month old with their grandparents. Her body was in Destin but so much of her mind was in Huntsville.

She had welcomed the break for three days. One morning as we ate breakfast on the balcony she commented, "It feels strange not changing a diaper or making snacks or hearing someone crying because they need to be held." Judy and I certainly didn't serve as substitutes. She had not heard, "Hey, Mommy…" for about 3 days now. When she reached over and began cutting up my steak at dinner the night before, I had to remind her that I was capable of doing that myself.

I was on vacation from my job those three days, but does a Mother ever have a vacation from hers? Even at the beach, you're still a Mother. Even when your children are 400 miles away, you're still a Mother. When we walked in stores to shop a little, the first department she began browsing in was the children's. Her first purchase of souvenirs was for the children.

The moms where I work fascinate me. As I see them arrive one by one they all clock in and begin their job, some before the sun is up. Fact of the matter is they've already put in a day's work before they even pulled in the parking lot. They've made lunches, dressed two or three kids, looked for homework papers that some how got lost between 9:00 pm and 6:30 am; fed the dog; got herself dressed; broken up an argument between siblings; wiped noses; provided needed counseling for heartaches here and there; packed extra clothes in case there's an "accident"; re-dressed herself because the accident got on her; loaded the van; gave lots of hugs and kisses; delivered children at appropriate locations; gave more hugs good-bye and said "have a good day"; drove to work and worked at least 8 hours. All of this every day, day in and day out, some with the help of their husband - some without.

I honestly don't know how they do it because when I leave at the end of my shift every day, what I do is pretty much to my choosing. If I go to the grocery store, anything I buy is strictly for me. Not so for these Moms. Their entire shopping list is all about the family.

My workday has ended but actually, it's high noon for them because that infamous question arises, "What's for dinner?" Their lists of duties continue with cooking, cleaning, hugging, doing homework, "refereeing" sibling rivalries, listening to "how your day went", more hugs and kisses until finally sometime before midnight they crawl in their bed, lay their head on the pillow, doze off to sleep only to hear, "Mommy, I don't feel good."

God gave us the incredible gift of our Moms. Only perfect gifts like a Mom could come from God. Mine, of course is the best in the world, but I'm fascinated to see how they never stop giving, doing, thinking, working, but most of all, loving. God gave you soft hearts but strong minds. Your endurance for pain brings precious children in the world who rely on you every minute of every day.

Do you ever outgrow the need for your Mother? In 1996, my grandmother Strickland passed away at the age of 96. Her service was in Anniston, Alabama and she was buried right next to Pop Strickland. On the way back to Huntsville, Mom, Dad and I stopped for dinner and Philip's family joined us. While eating, we began sharing wonderful memories of Mom Strickland and what a joy she was. Mother began to cry as we all became teary. Philip's middle daughter, Autrey was four years old at the time. She had not said much as she followed the conversation, but quietly jumped out of her chair, walked to Mother's seat, climbed in her lap, placed her hands on Mother's cheeks and asked, "Nanny, do you want your Mommy?"

"Yes, honey I do." Mother received more comfort from a four year old that day than anyone else.

I might have reached the age where I can tie my own shoe, pack my own lunch, separate my own laundry, blow my own nose and let Mom take a relaxing vacation.

But - I will never outgrow needing my Mommy.

My mommy and me on Mother's Day 1963. I was 20 months old.

MAY · WEEK THREE

I've Got The Power   John 3:16

Is it possible to feel completely alone in the second most populated city in the United States? There I was in a city of 9.8 million people and I honestly could not think of a time when I felt more alone and homesick than right then. I had just walked down a jetway following a flight from Fresno to Los Angeles. I had made wonderful friends during my short visit in Fresno, but the long journey home in the late night hours had just begun. As I faced a long layover in the LA airport, I began to think of ways to pass the time.

I had already talked to my best friend, Sisty, prior to leaving Fresno and with the different time zones, calling anyone back home was not a good idea. Eight o'clock in California means eleven o'clock in Chattanooga and ten o'clock at home, which is a little late on a Sunday night for chit chat. I was so homesick and missing everyone that I went as far as to listen to old messages just so I could hear the voices of people I love. In times like this, my laptop becomes my best friend. It's my connection to home and my way of feeling closer to the ones I love.

Walking through the LAX terminal, I began to search for an ideal location to sit with my laptop and wait for my next flight. Surprisingly, that was more challenging than I anticipated. I bet I walked through that concourse for 30 minutes trying to find a chair close to an electrical outlet. I was desperate. I wore myself out walking around looking and looking and then finally, someone left their spot and I immediately took his place. I plugged in and began connecting and writing. Whew! A connection to home. I was beginning to feel more southern by the minute.

I scanned Facebook and read what my friends had been up to the past few days. I read their comments of things I had posted from my trip to Yosemite National Park and how excited everyone was that I got to see that amazing place. I returned some e-mails and read through some work papers. I read local newspapers from home online and even listened to Dad's sermon on Mayfair's web page from that morning.

I couldn't help but notice others as they walked by me holding their laptops and it was obvious what they were searching for. They looked at every wall and up against every column at every gate but the only result of their search was frustration. One man sat by me and I said, "There's an outlet here with two plugs. I don't mind sharing."

He plopped down making some sarcastic comment about the LA airport being Amish and not having enough access to electrical outlets. I ignored him and went on about my business. All of that frustration and desperate search for one thing - POWER. A source of POWER. He and I both had tasks we wanted to accomplish and connections we wanted to make but they couldn't be made without POWER.

Are there times when you feel cut off? What's your source of power? Is it God? Is it His Spirit? Is it His people? Where do you search and where do you plug in for fulfillment?

Not long after the stranger sat down he shook the cord of his laptop, looked at the outlet and then asked me, "Are you getting any power from this outlet?" I had not even noticed, but I wasn't.

I was baffled and answered, "I guess not. I thought it was working, but I guess it's my battery and not the electrical source."

He snatched the cord of his laptop unplugging it from the outlet and in frustration walked off and said, "Well, good luck with that because your battery won't last long."

He's right. There I sat thinking I was all plugged in but in reality, I was relying on my own power. It wasn't long until the screen went blank and the power was gone. Back to searching for POWER.

Too often, I find myself becoming self-reliant and self-sufficient. I can handle this. I can do this on my own. But, the truth of the matter is, when it's all said and done, I'm completely powerless. Without God and His Spirit, I am nothing.

So often I hear others say, "I've got what I need and it's working just fine for me. I live a clean life. I give to the poor every now and then. I'm honest and I'm an all round good person. If that doesn't get me to heaven, nothing else will."

The problem with that theology is, you're relying on your own POWER. You're living off your own battery and sooner or later, that battery is going to die. Then what?

Paul wrote in Romans 5:6, that God sent His son to die for the ungodly. I like the translation from the NIV on that verse that says, "While we were still POWERLESS Christ died for the ungodly." POWERLESS. Salvation is nothing we can do on our own. Life is nothing we can do on our own. Our source of POWER and strength comes from God and only God.

Throughout this world, we see people desperately searching. They're alone and hurting. They're in need of a fulfillment that only God can give. Where do they plug in?

Thankfully, He's easier to find than an electrical outlet in LAX.

In fact, He found me.

MAY - WEEK FOUR

Anger - Is It Worth It?   Ephesians 4:32

Do you remember that old song we used to sing in church real often...

"Angry Words?" I bet you still remember the lyrics:

Angry words, O let them never
From the tongue, unbridled slip
May our heart's best impulse ever
Check them ere they soil the lip

Love one another thus saith the Savior
Children obey the Father's blest command

Remember how the ladies would sing the verses then the men with those strong bass voices would join in at the chorus? It's one of those songs that is taken directly from verses in the Bible. It's also one I've known all my life.

Sound advice, don't you agree? It's always amazing to me how the best of friendships can be damaged severely by one slip of the tongue or one moment of lost tempers. What can take years to build can be torn down in just a few moments. Homes are destroyed because someone can't control their anger and it volcanoes. I've heard law enforcement officers say most domestic disputes occur between 5:00 pm and 8:00 pm. I've wondered why but I think the reason is clear. That is when two tired bodies get home after a long day of work and a long day of tolerating the world and anger ignites. I know when I get home it would be very difficult to control my temper if I were "attacked" verbally as I walked in the door. Why do I do that? Why do I misdirect my anger on the one who deserves it the least? There are times when I can be more cordial to the greeter at Wal-Mart than I am to my own family.

It's almost laughable when you think about it. Anger can be a good thing. God permits us to be angry and Paul wrote about it in Ephesians 4:26: "In your anger, do not sin." In other words, get a grip on your anger. It's not a sin to be angry (thankfully) but, it's a sin when your anger controls you and gets out of hand.

Paul says in the next verse: "Do not let the sun go down when you are still angry." Why? Keep reading because he gives the answer to it all in verse 27: "and do not give the devil a foothold." Not dealing with it causes your anger to fester and nothing good can come from that.

There it is! There's your reason why anger can do serious damage to precious relationships. It gives that ol' devil an advantage; and when you give him the slightest advantage...Oh My...he'll take much, much more.

Sometimes, it's difficult to get things resolved before sundown. Maybe an apology was rendered but the recipient ignored it. Maybe you're angry about something that you absolutely have no control over and there's no way to resolve it. For example, the former employer that treated you like a second class citizen and eventually fired you knows you're angry, but really could care less. Maybe the spouse that kicked you to the curb is long gone with someone else and all you're left with is a bad memory and possibly children to support all by yourself. It makes perfect sense to be angry but until you let it go, you're the one that carries that burden - not the other party.

I'm thankful the Lord cut us some slack and allows us to get angry. I get angry when I watch the news and hear about someone abusing a child. I get angry when I see people throw away something precious like a marriage and their home that God ordained. I get angry when I hear of someone who rarely, if ever, abused their body but yet is inflicted with that horrible disease called cancer. I hate cancer. It angers me.

There are those who feel vindicated by bragging on their temper. "You don't want to see me lose my temper because that is a sight." Yeah, that's a characteristic you can certainly be proud of. My admiration is much stronger for that person who controls that anger and practices the act of meekness.

Sadly, I don't hear many people say, "I wish God would make me more meek." In our western hemisphere and southern way of thinking, we've destroyed the definition of meekness. It only rhymes with weakness. It's not a synonym. Meekness has strength, but it's controlled.

My brother, Philip, has a special talent of training horses. Mother and Dad had no idea when they chose the name "Philip" that it meant "lover of horses," or that their second son would grow up with a gift in working with them. He cares for several horses at his in-laws farm in Greenville, Alabama and at a location near his home in Guntersville, Alabama. Philip has had the task many times of breaking a horse. He tells me that it takes time until eventually you pull that rein and the horse realizes someone else is in control. The horse never loses the strength and ability to be forceful. The difference is, his will is controlled. Something else or someone else directs him.

It makes sense to get angry when you hear of things like child abuse or innocent people being mistreated. The problem comes when my anger comes over petty things and I fly off the handle and say things I regret. What will it matter 5 years from now? What will it matter 5 hours from now? Is it really important when you're looking at the big picture?

I hear parents share thoughts of regret as they remember when their children were small and they would get so angry over messes and spills and scattered toys throughout the house. Many little hearts were broken and spirits were crushed because of a silly bicycle left in the driveway or crayons crunched in the carpet resulting in words that did a lifetime of damage.

Anger. Is it worth it? Does it accomplish what you want it to accomplish? Is that how you want to be defined? I don't think so. Is being right and getting in the last word so important that relationships are destroyed?

Work through it and remember - *it just doesn't matter.*

MAY - WEEK FIVE

Catch Me, Daddy — Proverbs 3:5-6

It's the best example of trust I've ever seen. Many times when someone speaks of trust, the analogy given is the same. I was in Gulf Shores, Alabama enjoying a Memorial Day weekend with my friend, Donna Pate, and her girls. The weather was beautiful and we were enjoying the sun, sand and water. Donna had already settled in her chair with her book and I decided to take a morning walk. The sun was beaming from the clear blue sky but, it had not yet reached an uncomfortable level of heat. I smiled because summer had finally arrived. My favorite time of year.

It's usually in the morning that parents take young children to the beach. The sun is not as damaging and it's a great way for kids to burn off some energy. Walking down the beach, I loved watching the children run, squeal and play in the waves. Some had floats and boards as they splashed in the water while others began a serious task of building those massive sand castles. One little guy had buried his Dad in the sand then poured water over his head to cool him off.

My walk did have a purpose. I was in search of a Coke Machine. Not being a coffee drinker, I take my caffeine cold in the mornings and I needed a fix. As I scanned the pool sides of condominiums, I finally spotted that big red sign reading, "COKE". I walked up the steps, went around the pool and made my purchase. The caffeine headache left me immediately and my parched throat was quenched.

Walking back to the beach, I noticed a man standing in the middle of the pool with outstretched arms. As you know, there's really no longer a "deep end" for swimming pools - at least not for grown-ups over 5 and a half feet tall. This man stood at least six feet and he easily cleared the five feet level in the middle of the pool. He looked like a patient man as he watched his daughter's indecisiveness, but quickly, that patience was wearing thin.

A little girl, no older than three, stood by the pool. Her little pink bathing suit matched the flip-flops lying beside a beach bag near a chair. She had blonde hair and curls that some grown women pay hundreds of dollars for, but hers were God given. I took a seat in one of the chairs by a table as I sipped on my Coke. I didn't want to miss this moment as this Dad was not going to give up.

"Come on, Honey, " the dad pleaded with the child. "Just jump right here and Daddy is going to catch you, I promise."

She didn't say a word. Her lips barely grasped the tip of her index finger. She shuffled her feet every now and then and swung her hips from side to side. Her eyes scanned the water, then she studied her Daddy's face. She again scanned the water, then her Daddy, back to the water, then her Daddy and finally took a deep breath. You could read the anticipation on her face. She wanted to jump but fear prevented her from making the plunge.

I guess the reason this scene fascinated me so much is because it looked SO familiar. Many years ago, (emphasis on the many) I actually remember standing on the side of a swimming pool. My hair was blonde, but I'm not sure I had the curls.

I clearly remember planting my brown eyes directly into Daddy's brown eyes and hearing his pleas, "Honey, jump and I'll catch you." His arms were outstretched. There was no doubt in my mind that he'd catch me. But, just like that little girl, something held me back. What if I went under? What if he missed? Was he teasing me and not really going to catch me?

Trust! There are times when we have absolutely no idea what the future holds. Something has changed in our lives or plans we laid out didn't transpire the way we thought they would and our vision of the future is grossly distorted. Where will I be in five years? Who will be with me?

It's not always easy. There are the fears of doubt that pop in our head as we scan the arms of our Father. Does He really hear me? Others have let me down - is He going to do the same.

Trust is earned. Nothing validates that trust more than when I allow Him to catch me when I'm not real sure about the jump. Just like Daddy used to do, He stands there waiting patiently but yet pleading, "Come on! I'll catch you. I promise." Every time I jumped, He caught me.

Abraham can vouch for that. In Genesis 12:1 God commands him (at that time called Abram), "Leave your country, your people and your father's household and go to a land that I'll show you." Not real specific direction there, is it? He tells him to pack it up, leave what you've always known and go. I'm not going to tell you where, just go.

Later, God commands Abraham to step out a little farther in his faith in what is probably one of the most emotional chapters in the Bible. Genesis 22 brings a tear to my eye every time I read it. "Take your son, your ONLY son and sacrifice him as a burnt offering on one of the mountains." Yes, that's correct, Abraham. Take that boy, the one God promised you'd have and kill him as a burnt sacrifice to God.

Remember verse 5 of that chapter as Abraham and Isaac approach the mountain? Abraham tells the servants to stay while he and the boy go and worship, then he tells them, WE will worship and WE will return. Abraham had no idea how but he trusted God and knew his boy would not die. He trusted God's promises.

Oh, the questions from that chapter! How did Abraham continue to reassure Isaac of God's provisions as the innocent question came, "Father, where's the sacrifice?" How did an old man like Abraham get a young, strong, teenage boy on that altar? Was there a shade of doubt or fear in Abraham's mind as he pulled the knife out and even held it in the position to plunge it into his son's body?

The only answer to these questions is God kept His promise. Abraham jumped and God caught him.

That little girl finally took the big leap and just as her precious little painted toe nails touched that water, that Daddy caught his baby girl, hugged her and laughed with her as she finally overcame her fear.

Catch me, God. I'm going to jump.

"Nothing compares to the promise I have in You."

JUNE - WEEK ONE

The Mask Will Appear — James 1:23

"Delta Flight 6402 non-stop service from Birmingham to New York-Laguardia is now boarding. Please have your boarding pass ready..." The announcement came as I gathered my bag and prepared to get on the aircraft. My friend, Melisa had just dropped me off at the airport. I told her as we drove in, "It's not real comforting to think, when you're about to get on an airplane, one of the last words you see is 'terminal.'" She was amused, even at 5:00 in the morning.

I boarded the plane, found my seat, buckled my seat belt and got ready for take-off. Others around me did the same; some placed their bags in the overhead compartment while others waited as they found their seat assignment. In less than 2 1/2 hours, we'll be in New York City.

The flight attendant who greeted us as we boarded made several trips up and down the aisle assisting passengers and performing her duties prior to take-off. She gave instructions and explanations - something she no doubt does several times a day. I always feel somewhat sorry for flight attendants. They stand before the group of passengers and recite the same speech that you hear at every take-off but no one pays the least bit of attention to them. They direct you to the guide placed in the bin in front of you and ask you to please read these instructions. Maybe a first time flyer will peek at it but otherwise, everyone ignores the instruction. They point out the exit signs and assure you that should any unforeseen event occur, there is adequate lighting that directs you to the exit.

I'm always amused when they tell me that my seat is also a flotation device. Not only does it support me as I sit, but I could use it to ride the waves in Destin if I wanted to. Anytime I'm flying west I'm always intrigued at the fact that my seat is a flotation device. I think of my favorite comedian James Gregory who says, "I'm flying

52

from Georgia to Oklahoma. Don't give me something that's going to float. Give me something that will bounce in a corn field." AGREED!

The flight attendant then provides some valuable information that I think we all rely on, whether we're on an airplane or not. Let me paraphase what she says:

In the event of an emergency, the mask will appear.

Sounds like a good plan, huh? How many times in our daily lives do emergencies come up and PRESTO - there's our mask? Ready and available to hide anything. Don't let anyone see the real us. No problems here. No baggage in this life.

How many of us on Sunday mornings dress for church, wear our best outfits, put on our best smiles, give the kids a good spit wash on the way, making sure those Kool-Aid mustaches are gone and walk in with huge smiles on our faces? Fellow members shake our hand and ask that weekly common question, "How y'all doin?"

In our best southern tone (using about five syllables in a one syllable word) we all answer the same way, "FINE!" "We're FINE!"

The truth of the matter is we're not all FINE. Some of us are carrying more pain than any words could express. One of the best kept secrets on your church pew is your pain. It's hidden well. Maybe it's an anniversary of a loved one's death. Everyone else has grieved and "gotten over it," but for you the pain is still as fresh as that morning's first cup of coffee.

Maybe it's a troubled marriage at home but you wouldn't dare make that known because nobody would understand. You need advice and you need prayers from others but who among all of these strong Christians can relate? How in the world could you let someone know something like that? Real Christians don't have troubled marriages. You better make sure that mask is on good and tight for that one.

The Bible tells us in James 5 "Confess your sins one to another and pray for each other…" Can we really do this? Surely my sin is far more heinous than anyone elses. No one could be as sinful as me. No one else is struggling with addiction; no one else has a rebellious child; no one else is so lonely that every night their pillow is soaking wet from tears. It's only you and luckily that emergency mask is right there!

Somehow, the masks have got to come off. I think the Apostle John blows the whistle on us and exposes who we really are. In I John, he spends much of the book instructing us to love God and each other, but you know what comes first? Admitting your own sin. Admitting that you're not perfect. Admitting that we ALL have issues.

He begins the book in I John 1:8, "If we claim to be without sin, we deceive everybody around us because we wear a mask." No! Wait! That's not what it says. It says "…we deceive God because we've got Him fooled, too." NO! Look again. It reads "If we claim to be without sin, we deceive OURSELVES and the TRUTH is not in us." Sooner or later, the mask fades and the truth is exposed. We're only fooling ourselves if we think we can hide it.

I truly believe that through inspiration, John is instructing us to "Get Real!" Be yourself and no matter what's underneath that mask that you think hides it all, God loves you anyway. That pain that you think no one can accept and relate to, God can. He sees the tears in your eyes and hears you when you cry.

Lose the mask and maybe others will do the same.

JUNE - WEEK TWO

Hand Over The Wheel — Romans 8:12-13

The summer of 1972 is so clear in my mind. I was 10 years old, we were living in Chattanooga and it was the peak season for "GOSPEL MEETINGS." Some churches called them "revivals" but we in the Churches of Christ referred to them as "GOSPEL MEETINGS." Every congregation had one and prepared for months to make it a success. You had to have an enthusiastic song leader, a fiery preacher, a full baptistry, plenty of food for "dinner on the ground" and lots of air in your lungs to sing 634 verses of "Just As I Am."

Living in Chattanooga, we were only two hours or less from many destinations for these "gospel meetings." During that summer, Dad had nine scheduled back to back. This was back in the days when the meeting started on Sunday morning and continued through Friday night. Dad was preaching for Brainerd Church of Christ at the time and their Sunday morning services started at 9:15. Being on eastern time, he preached that service and just after the invitation song, he would leave and drive to his scheduled meeting - usually in towns located in Tennessee or on Sand Mountain in North Alabama.

Those locations are on central time so, Dad was able to arrive just as their services began. After dinner on the ground and sometime during the afternoon singing, Dad would drive back to Chattanooga, preach for the evening service at Brainerd then drive back to the meeting because those services usually started at 7:30. He would then preach the next five nights, going home one day during the week to take care of duties with Brainerd, then preparing on Saturday to do it all again the next day. Are you tired just reading that itinerary? He was much younger then...

As kids, it was always a treat when Dad would take us with him on those trips. We would take turns going with him and would love staying in the motel and eating with the members each night. It was amazing how evangelistic I could be when Dad stayed at a motel with a swimming pool. Dad did a lot of driving that summer and needed something easy on gas. He bought a 1967 Volkswagen "bug" that was previously owned by Sisty's family. I'd love to have that car back. I never remember it missing a step as we drove through those hills of Tennessee and up and down I-24 and I-59. A tank of gas? about four bucks.

Those were special times with Dad and I cherish those memories. Every now and then on our way back to the motel or to Chattanooga, Dad would let me sit in his lap and "drive" the car. I would steer the wheel and move my hand over to pull the gear down as Dad stepped on the clutch. I was just a 10 year old little girl, but in my mind I felt like I was 25 because I was driving that car and in control.

IN CONTROL! Yep - that's how I felt. I was the one making the choices of which lane we were in, which direction we were going and where we were to turn. It was in MY hands...or was it? Far too often we think we're in full control of our lives and we determine which direction it all goes when in reality, someone else is truly in control.

As grown up as I felt and as good of a driver I thought I was, little did I know Dad had his hands on the bottom of the steering wheel. He was the one making the determinations of direction. His foot controlled the speed and when we stopped.

Some of us just have to be control freaks. Do I dare use the word freaks? Yes- I'm going to stick with that one. FREAKS! I go back to the analogy of driving - if I'm riding with someone and I know exactly where I'm going but they do not, it makes me nuts! It's all I can do to not push them out of the way and say, "Just let me do it." Some managers and supervisors in the work place handicap their employees when they do not allow them to do a task themselves and learn from mistakes.

Throughout the book of Romans, Paul stresses to us that something far greater leads us and directs our lives as Christians. When we became Christians, we received that gift known as the Holy Spirit.

Have you ever noticed that many times in the Bible when the topic of being "spirit filled" is discussed it is compared to being drunk? On the day of Pentecost when the apostles were speaking in tongues and preaching to the people gathered in Jerusalem what was the accusation? "THEY'RE DRUNK!" Peter stood before them in Acts 2 and said, "We're not drunk but rather we are filled with the spirit."

Paul wrote in Eph. 5:18 to not be drunk with wine but rather be filled with the spirit. The reason the state of Alabama, or any other state in this country, does not want me drunk when I'm driving is because something else is controlling that vehicle - not me. That's why they call it "driving under the influence."

The Holy Spirit should be our influence. The Holy Spirit is the one that controls our lives and directs our steps. That's why when you feel compelled to make an apology, you make it. You feel like losing your temper and lashing out at some deserving soul but, the Spirit compels you to refrain. So you hold back.

Being Spirit filled starts when you let go. You surrender that stubborn will and realize, "Lord, I can't control this life without You." The blessing of it all is His way is far more peaceful. He still gives us the choice to go any direction that we want to take. Yes, there are detours and yes there are bumps in the road and sometimes we feel we are absolutely the only ones on the road. But, He's still there. He's still got the wheel in His hands.

Let it go! Give it to Him - and enjoy the ride.

JUNE - WEEK THREE

I Need To Call My Dad   Romans 8

Stepping out of his pick-up truck, he approached the scene of the accident. His son stood beside me and there were others standing near by. A mist of rain blew through the air but it really wasn't enough to bring out the umbrellas. The son was shaking and the scrapes on his knees were bleeding.

It was easy to tell that the man getting out of that pick-up was the boy's father. They were the same height and built exactly alike. I was tempted to look at the son and tell him, "That's what you'll look like in 25 years."

He instructed his son just like a father. "Have your license and insurance ready when the police get here." He investigated the son's car like a father. "Well, I'm sure State Farm will total this." He asked questions like a father, "Did anyone see this happen? Was there another vehicle involved?" He informed the police like a father, "We use State Farm insurance. Here's the card. I'll call the wrecker service and have them come pick up the car."

Let me fill you in on the events. If you drive from the Hampton Cove area in Huntsville to Jones Valley, you travel on Cecil Ashburn Drive that cuts through a mountain close to Green Mountain. It's a gorgeous route with a breath taking view of south Huntsville. Many clear days you can see Marshall Space Center on Redstone Arsenal and The Space and Rocket Center. It is absolutely beautiful in the fall on those crisp clear days and the color of the trees make it difficult to keep your eyes on the road.

It was an early Friday evening in June and I was running an errand to that side of the mountain. It had started to sprinkle and then drizzle but never a full down pour of rain. More rain was on the way so it was darker than usual at 7:20 pm. I had several things on my mind as I was preparing for the weekend. I needed to run by Belk and pick up Daddy's Father's Day present, then get it wrapped. Other things were running through my mind because I wanted to make sure I had bought the right card. I wonder if Philip and Kim are coming over with the kids? I think Lucy plays tennis the next day...all of these random lists going through my head.

As my car climbed the hill and the music rang through my speakers, my jaw dropped. A beige Mercury Sable (older model) traveling east bound began to fishtail and the back end of the car was headed straight toward me. Quickly, I jerked the wheel, sped up and moved to the far side of the two lane road. If you've ever driven over Cecil Ashburn Drive, you realize you have few options of places to pull over. While traveling west, a huge drop off from the mountain was to my left and a rocky mountain side to my right.

I slipped ahead just as the Mercury passed by and then the rollover began. The vehicle rolled at least three times landing back on the tires and then began sliding backwards until finally coming to a stop up against the rocky mountainside. That horrible sound of steel and tires screeching could be heard throughout the valley. No smoke, but a lot of broken glass and vehicle parts scattered over the road.

I had already jumped out of my car and was in full stride running down the hill toward the driver. My trembling fingers dialed "9-1-1" and as best I could, I gave directions to the dispatcher. My mind expected the worst as I got closer to the driver and dodged the glass in my path.

He was a kid. OK- probably 22 or 23, but to me, a kid. He had already crawled out of the car and was pacing as he tried to catch his breath. I had never seen this young man in my life, but in a split second I began thanking God he was alive. He sat down on one of the rocks. I ran to the car and made sure there were no other passengers. EMPTY! Thank, God.

I knelt down beside him and ordered, *"LOOK AT ME!"*

He was shaking all over but there was no bleeding anywhere from his head. His eyes looked fine and the only injury appeared to be where the glass cut his knees and blood was pouring from both of them. He talked coherently and others had stopped by then. I ran to my car and got a towel hooked to my golf bag so he could blot the blood.

The lights from the police car and paramedics lit up the night. He insisted he was fine but they began to treat him, just to make sure. He looked at me and said:

"I need to call my Dad. May I use your phone?"

I handed him the phone as the paramedics continued to examine him. He made the call and within five minutes, the white pick-up truck belonging to his father, pulled up to the scene. Stepping out of his truck, he walked straight to his son, put his arms around him and the two of them cried. I tried fighting it but once I saw one of the paramedics wiping his eyes, I cried too. He held his son and asked him over and over again, *"Are you OK?"*

This time he sounded like a Dad! He protected like a Dad. He comforted like a Dad. He forgave when the son apologized for tearing up the car like a Dad. He loved his son like a Dad.

I'm thankful God is our Father. That's what the Bible tells us in Isaiah 63:16. But, to put it in Alabama language (as Dad says), He is our Dad. The New Testament uses the word "Abba", which means "Daddy". Paul tells us He made us His sons. (Galatians 4:6)

Our Father instructs like a Father, informs like a Father, and we're made in our Father's image. What more could you ask for?

But, thankfully, He loves us, just like a Dad.

JUNE - WEEK FOUR

Parenting Is Not For Wimps   *Proverbs 22:6*

While standing in the kitchen of my parent's house pouring a Coke in a "to go" cup, I carried on a conversation with my brother, Philip, who was in the bedroom down the hall. It was a warm Monday afternoon - the third day of September, Labor Day, and a day Philip and his wife, Kim, had dreamed of for many years. Kim had given birth to a precious baby boy two days prior and Philip was running errands before he went back to the hospital. It was time for him to carry his wife and new baby boy home.

For a minute or so, I didn't hear Philip's voice and then I heard sniffing and what sounded like crying. I walked down the hall and asked, "Are you OK?" I'm sure exhaustion had set in and emotions were off the chart.

Philip wiped his eyes, regained his composure and announced to me, "They're going to make us take him home. I have a son and I'm scared to death."

I'm not sure my words of encouragement made him feel better but I gave it my best shot reminding him, "Hey, this is what we all prayed for. He's healthy. He's just cute as he can be. Besides, whatever you mess up, Kim will fix." I thought a little humor would lighten the mood. That was in 1990. Philip and Kim took that little boy home from the hospital and in the coming years added two little girls to their family.

I remembered that moment with Philip as I sat in the gymnasium of Guntersville High School. Our family, along with Kim's family anxiously waited to hear that little boy's name: Benjamin Philip Bradley. We all applauded and belted out a "YEE HAW" as we watched his 6'5" body walk in front of the crowd, shake hands with the principal and school superintendent and accept his high school diploma.

How did those years pass so quickly? It was just last week, or so it seems, that Ben was running through the house in his Winnie the Pooh underwear and singing

My brother, Philip, graduated with his Masters degree in Old Testament History in 1996. He's a great preacher, husband, and an amazing dad to Ben, Autrey, and Lucy

"Here is Noah...here is his boat..." OK - not last week but maybe a few years ago. Thirteen years of field trips, Sunday School classes, Little League, a broken leg from middle school football, science projects, tennis tournaments and championships and everything else that goes with it, Ben was ready for college. His hard work in school and talents as a tennis player had earned him a scholarship to Harding University. Whatever it was that Philip thought he'd mess up, he didn't. He and Kim sure did a lot of things right.

Parenthood! I don't know how some of you do it. I heard parenting illustrated this way. A man sat in the upper deck of a professional baseball stadium with his four year old son. It was his son's very first game and how eager the Dad was for his son to catch the passion for the game. For years he had taught him all about different players, the history of the game, the rules, the strategy and everything else he knew about baseball.

Then it happened. Right there in the upper deck here it came. A foul ball, sky high and in reach of those upper deck fans. This dad gasped for breath and watched that ball come directly toward him and his boy. The dad leaned over the rail of the third level upper deck, stretched out his arm as far as he could. The crowd watched in horror and in fear that he would flip right over that rail. Just in time, he pulls in the ball and steps back to safety. The crowd ROARS with cheers and a congratulatory applause! He holds the ball up in triumph. The television cameras pan immediately to his glorious face and no doubt, his outstanding catch will make the highlight feature on ESPN.

What an accomplishment! He immediately turned to his boy hoping to see admiration and an expression of hero worship. The boy just stood there not really knowing what to think. The dad proudly handed him his prize baseball and no doubt envisioned his son one day putting that ball in a special case to keep forever. Instead, the boy simply glanced at the ball and did what he was taught to do with any baseball - HE THREW IT! Right back on the field the ball landed, and the father almost cried.

That's parenting. You risk your life, you reach as far as you can and in your mind you're a hero... only to watch the would be worshipper chunk your efforts back to the field. Just throwing it all away.

Parenting is not for wimps. It's not for anyone who is weak spiritually. I can't imagine anyone trying to raise a child in this day and time without spending constant time in prayer and consulting God's word for guidance. So, what's the secret to raising a child in the 21st century? What do you do when you feel scared like my brother did?

Consult the experts. Go ahead and read all of those books by child psychologists. But before doing all of that, get in The Word. Start reading the Word of God and make it part of your every day conversation. Pray with your kids. Make every day a day that draws you all closer to our Father. Then one day that child will hold that "baseball" up proudly, and never throw it back on the field.

Before you can say "play ball", you'll be their "MVP" - Most Valuable Parent."

JULY - WEEK ONE

Call The LifeGuard *Proverbs 3: 5-6*

It was the Fourth of July, a time when we all celebrate our nation's birthday. Americans celebrate this holiday in a variety of ways - cook-outs, family reunions, boat rides at the lake, fireworks...lots of traditions. My celebration was a little different this year as I opted to stay home and not get in the crowds and just rest. After a tough week at work, I needed some time at home. To be honest, it wasn't much different from any other summer Saturday.

After some time soaking the sun by the pool, I got cleaned up, put on my favorite shorts and t-shirt and ventured off to the grocery store. Usually dressed like that I pray I don't see anybody I know because my hair is not fixed and I don't have on a drop of make-up.

Walking into Kroger a man noticed my t-shirt which read "SEASIDE". It was a souvenir purchase from a previous trip to Seaside, Florida. The man commented as I passed him, "I bet you wish you were there right now."

I smiled and replied, "Yes sir, more than you know." He had no idea I had just been thinking about Fourth of July celebrations in the past at the beach. Memories had flooded my mind of those years at my friend Lois's beach house and the fun we had. I recalled 1985 when about 30 of us spent the Fourth down there. This Fourth I spent it wishing I didn't have to work for a living and could just live at the beach year round. The man then asked, "Have you been to Seaside lately?"

I explained that we usually stay a mile away from Seaside in Sea Grove and my friends and I were down there last month. "We love it down there."

He then asked, "Do you know if there's a lifeguard on the beach in that area?"

I had to stop and think for a minute and responded, "Well, sir, I never really noticed one. I've noticed the guys who set out the chairs and umbrellas are around but I'm not sure they're lifeguards."

A lifeguard? I didn't see a big tall white oversized chair on the beach with a red flotation device like they carry on "Baywatch". I didn't notice pretty people running down the beach in red bathing suits ready to rescue someone. I didn't see some muscular young guy with the white sun block on his nose wearing a t-shirt that read "LIFEGUARD". I don't remember Mary, Regina or Melisa commenting about seeing a lifeguard our entire trip.

Maybe the reason we didn't notice a lifeguard on the beach is because at the time we didn't need one. Perhaps if someone became distressed while swimming in the gulf, out of nowhere a hero would have appeared and saved the drowning soul. As I think about it, even if the presence of a lifeguard had been obvious, we still would have ignored him/her because there was no need for that service.

I think there are other areas in our lives when we completely ignore something, unless we need it. Insurance policies are ignored...until we need them. Flight attendants are ignored...until we need them. Sometimes it's that way with people in our lives. Doesn't it annoy you when the only time you hear from someone is when they need something? Maybe you have a "friend" whom you enjoy hearing from, but it seems events are quite one sided and the only time you hear from that person is when they have a question or need a favor.

Sometimes that describes our relationship with God. While His presence is obvious in His creation, we choose to ignore Him and go about our lives as if we are self-sufficient. But, sooner or later, it happens. Out of the blue, lightning strikes and immediately our lives turn to chaos. The waves get higher and the riptides are pulling us under and away from safety. The pain is so deep and we're just not sure which way to turn. We become desperate and cry out, "OH GOD! HELP ME!"

He's right there. He reaches out and pulls us from danger and cradles us in His arms.

We will never out give God. We will never be able to "out do" Him. He's never asked that of us. All He asks is for us to acknowledge Him and to be thankful, even if you don't notice He's there. And maybe if we would acknowledge Him more often, those storms wouldn't be so scary.

Don't forget: no matter where you are, your lifeguard is always on duty.

JULY - WEEK TWO

What's Your Thorn?   2 Corinthians 12:9

Have you ever noticed some areas in the Bible that kind of leave you hanging? The story of the Prodigal Son is a prime example in Luke 15. The Prodigal makes his way home and is welcomed by the father with open arms. A party is thrown with family, friends and lots of good food as they welcome this wayward boy back to the fold. The father ends up having to plead with this Prodigal's elder brother to come in the house, accept your brother, forgive your brother and join the party. Does he go inside? We're not told.

A few chapters later in Luke 18, a young man who said he had kept every rule and every word of the Ten Commandments walked away from Jesus after he was told that he'd have to sell all of his riches and follow Christ. Did he ever have a change of heart and eventually follow Christ? We're not told.

Acts 28 is the ending of an incredible book of history as we learn about the early years of the church, Saul's conversion, Saul's name changing to Paul, and Paul putting his life on the line to share the gospel throughout the region. Many times a story or book will end with statements like "and they lived happily ever after" or "there he died and was buried" or something like that. The book of Acts ends with Paul preaching in Rome and the verse reads, "Boldly and without hindrance he preached the kingdom of God and taught about the Lord Jesus Christ." No indication as to what happened to Paul - no clear picture as to how he died or when he died. No documentation of what happened to the people he preached to, or if they prospered.

One of the most curious verses in the Bible is found in 2 Corinthians 12 when Paul speaks of his thorn in the flesh. The thorn in the flesh! Now that's quite a question. Talk about being left hanging - Paul gives little if any clue of what that thorn in the flesh might have been. I've asked many experts and friends whom I know study the Bible closely for their opinion of what was Paul's thorn in the flesh. Recently, I brought up the topic to Mom and Dad and asked what they thought was Paul's thorn in the flesh. Jokingly I said, "Well, we know Paul wasn't married so that narrows it down."

Mother quickly added that some believe at one time in his life Paul was married. Dad chimed in, "Yes, he was married and her name was Grace because God told him 'My GRACE is sufficient for you." (insert rolling of eyes here)

Many years ago while I was living in Birmingham, I asked my preacher, Wayne Kilpatrick what he thought Paul's thorn in the flesh was. "That's easy!" Wayne answered. "It was a Deacon!" They need to add more comedian classes to the curriculum in preacher's schools.

That thorn in the flesh - was it a physical condition? Migraine headaches? Epilepsy? Malaria? Was his eyesight not completely restored after that incident on the Road to Damascus? Did Paul have some sort of speech impediment?

Was it a spiritual condition? Was there a temptation that Paul didn't feel he could overcome? Were there opponents hindering Paul from carrying out the will of God to spread the gospel? So many questions but no definitive answers. At least, I sure don't know the answer. What I do know is that Paul asked God three times to remove this thorn in the flesh. THREE TIMES! At least he was persistent.

Going back to the examples I gave - maybe the reason the Lord left us hanging and doesn't reveal "the rest of the story" is because He wants us to write our own ending. He wants us to put our own hearts and lives in that elder brother in Luke 15. We're the ones to decide if he goes in and joins the party. Perhaps it's up to the church today to write the 29th chapter of Acts. Are there things in our lives that we consider our own thorn in the flesh that we can insert in the blank left in 2 Corinthians 12? Do any of us have a physical handicap we've asked God to heal or take away? Have you asked God over and over for something you want so badly but you're beginning to feel He lost your address or hasn't heard your plea?

No matter what you insert in the blank or no matter what you label as your thorn in the flesh, the answer is the same. Yep - the same exact answer He gave Paul. When God explained to him (and I like the way it's interpreted in The Message) "My grace is enough, it's all you need. My strength comes into its own in your weakness." The answer fits no matter if it's Paul's thorn in the flesh or mine.

I'm not there yet or at least I'm not consistent with it. For some things I can readily accept that God's grace is sufficient but when it comes to those deep, heart wrenching, down on my knees "please oh please oh please, God" - I'm not there yet. I mean, we're told that if we ask God for what we want, live a good life, go to church, treat others kindly, don't smoke, don't chew, don't go with boys who do...then God will give you what you want. Especially if you're asking for something that's not immoral, illegal or unethical. Why wouldn't He say yes?

Where did we get such a bogus religious philosophy like that? When did God become Santa Claus? Be a good girl and good things will happen. I take comfort in knowing that I'm not the only one who struggles with this thought process and others, like me, haven't reached that point in their Christianity. Others I know with a physical handicap have asked God to take it away but yet, their struggle continues. We pray for loved ones to be healed from their illnesses, yet they die. We ask God to grant us our desires and deep down we truly feel this will make us a better Christian and help us grow closer to Him. Paul reasoned and bargained the same way but, God said no.

How do I get there? How do I accept God's grace and know that He truly will help me deal with my own thorn in the flesh? Just like Paul, I need to change my focus. Back to 2 Corinthians 12:10 (once again from The Message) "Once I heard that God's grace was sufficient, I was glad to let it happen. I quit focusing on the handicap and began appreciating the gift. It was a case of Christ's strength moving in on my weakness."

In other words, Paul realized it wasn't about him but rather it's about Him. I've got to do the same thing. Somehow, I've got to grow to the point where I know God knows best. He will give me what I need - not always what I want. I trust Him. I surrender to the fact that it's all about Him. He's not going to withhold anything good that will bring me closer to Him. Accept God's grace.

That's what it will take for me to write my own happy ending.

JULY - WEEK THREE

I'm Thirsty — Psalm 42: 1-2

The summer of 2011 was hot in Alabama. So was 2010. So was 2009 and 2008 and 2007. I still have a clear memory of summer 1980 and it was a hot one. After 50 years, I've never seen a cool, comfortable summer in Alabama. I guess that's why it annoys me when people complain about the heat. "Whew, it sure is hot."

Well, of course it's hot. You're in Alabama and it's July. It gets hot around here every summer.

One of the issues that we have to deal with during the hot summers is the lack of rain. In 2007, we had one of the worst droughts I had ever seen. We had an unusual freeze in early April and even had snow flurries the night before Easter. All of the spring blooms, the dogwoods, Bradford Pears, azaleas and many flowers froze and our colors weren't as pretty as usual. Once the front came through and everything melted, we got little if any rain for the rest of the spring and summer.

On hot summer days, I am in search of a swimming pool. My friend, Mary Milam is always gracious to allow me to come to her house, enjoy her pool, drink a Dr. Pepper and have a good visit. We will float in her pool for hours, soak up the sun and solve all the world's problems. It's the next best thing to being at the beach.

Each spring and summer, Mary has a beautiful backyard. Her husband, Bobby keeps the grass mowed and Mary plants beautiful flowers all around the pool and back deck. The colors just add to the beauty of her pool and compliment the relaxing atmosphere of her backyard.

Mary has shown me that having a beautiful yard full of flowers and plants takes a lot of hard work. When I arrived for our pool time together, there stood Mary in her swimsuit, holding the garden hose and allowing the water to replenish the parched dirt around the flowers. "Cindi, there's no telling what our water bill is going to be this month. If we don't get some rain soon, I'm just going to have let these flowers wilt."

One July Saturday, Mary and Bobby were gone to a family reunion out of town. They're always so kind to allow me to make myself at home, even when they're gone, so I set up poolside and enjoyed the sun. When I arrived, I noticed Mary's flowers were wilted and in dire need of water. It was no problem for me to turn on the hose and spray those petunias and impatiens with a good dose of cold water.

The sun was so hot and the weather man had predicted we would hit close to 100 degrees that day. Those flowers were feeling every bit of that heat, but when the first drop of water hit those pedals, new life went in to those flowers. The ones that were drooping, immediately perked up. The ones that were dried out and almost wilted began to look lively and moist.

Are you thirsty? Has your spiritual life ever felt like dry, parched dirt and you've not been refreshed in many weeks? Has your faith dried up to the point where it seems there is no life to it and no possibility of reviving it?

In John 4, Jesus met a woman who was thirsty and had no idea that her source of quenching that thirst was in vain. She drew water from a well but little did she know that the water from the well was lifeless. She thought it served its purpose and fulfilled her needs but she had no idea how that one day changed her life for all eternity. She met the very one who would completely quench her thirst for a lifetime.

She thought he was just a man sitting by the well. It threw her off when this MAN asked her, a WOMAN for a drink of water. Men didn't speak to women back then. It also surprised her that a JEW would speak to her, a SAMARITAN. Jews hated Samaritans. He then told her to do something, and He knew good and well what her response would be:

"Go get your husband."

Whew, Lord. That's a tough one for her. She answered Him honestly:

"I don't have a husband."

"That's right. You've had five husbands and the man you're living with now isn't your husband."

It had to blow her mind when the Lord read her life like an open book. He knew her better than any one she had ever come in contact with. He knew she had been in many beds, but had never found rest. He knew she had made love, but had never known true love. He knew she had been in many weddings but had never experienced the commitment of a marriage. He knew she was aware of God - but she never knew the peace of the Father.

Every day, for who knows how long, she walked to that well and drew what she thought would quench her thirst. Jesus told her, "You come to a well for water. I know of a spring that will give you LIVING water and you'll never be thirsty again."

She was intrigued. She asked if he was a prophet and then asked, "Where is this spring so I can get this LIVING water?" Well water is still and stagnant. Jesus is a spring of water; a spring that is constantly moving; a spring that is pure and the water is cool and refreshing. Yeah, that's what she wanted. That's what she had been looking for in all the wrong places.

Just like Alabama summers, the world can dry out our faith and wilt away our hope and feeling of assurance. The same water that was offered to that woman in John 4 is still available today. Just like Mary's flowers, your faith and your life will be renewed and revived. He offers it to you and me, and just like He promised her, the same promise holds true - you'll never thirst again.

Bring Him your bucket. He'll fill it up.

JULY - WEEK FOUR

A Cup of Grandmother's Advice   2 Tim. 4:12

A business trip took me to Montgomery, Alabama one July week. I didn't get back to Montgomery real often so I was looking forward to being in familiar territory and seeing some relatives. The temps were high but I had a comfortable bed and cool air conditioning at my Aunt Nita's house. Staying with my aunt makes a business trip less lonely. She lives about 200 yards away from the house where my grandparents lived for many years. The house had been recently sold and it made me sad that I wasn't able to go there anymore. As I was leaving Montgomery, I drove by the house and couldn't help but explore. It was obvious that the previous owners had already vacated the house as it was empty. I pulled in the driveway and in a split second, I felt like I was 16 again.

Getting out of my car in that driveway felt comfortable and familiar. I peeked through the windows and walked to the side of the house to the back door. To my surprise, the door was unlocked and I stepped in. I took a risk walking inside but it was a risk worth taking.

I walked in the den. The decor was different but oh my, the memories. It was only natural that I had a Dr. Pepper in my hand as I stood in that room. There was total silence as I looked at the empty rooms. Total silence - except for the noises that I could hear in my head.

I heard voices; familiar voices of family members as stories were being told but mostly my ears rang with laughter. Lots and lots of laughter. At gatherings, the seven grandchildren would sit at one table together and after dinner, tell stories, reminisce and laugh until we hurt.

I could smell food - maybe turkey on a Thanksgiving day or ham out of the oven on Christmas Eve. My grandmother made the best potato salad you ever put in your mouth and the smell of eggs, potatoes and whatever else she put in it to make it fabulous came to mind.

I stepped back in the den and saw the fireplace. To my surprise, it was still standing. The mantle that once hung over that fireplace had been replaced. The senior pictures of us grandchildren were once displayed there and I remember the sense of accomplishment I felt on the day I brought mine.

I looked in that empty den and recalled how Wo's furniture was arranged. She had a sofa against the wall and that was where she usually sat. Granddaddy's recliner was on the right side of the room with his ash tray standing right next to the right arm rest. I honestly think I spent more time in that house than I did in our house during the years we lived in Montgomery. I went to their house after school and spent many weekends there, mostly because Wo would let me watch "Dallas" on Friday nights.

I stepped out of the den and down the hall to the first room on the right. I hesitated and let the memories flood as I stepped in Wo's bedroom. In this room, I smelled her perfume, Channel #5. Just to the right in her bedroom was the bathroom and her vanity and one of many closets in that house that were full of her clothes.

I heard music as I stood in that room. The space where she kept her stereo was in the right corner of her bedroom. The tunes from Conway Twitty, George Jones, Elvis and many others rang through my ears. There was always a stack of records lined up ready to play her favorites.

"Hey, Dahlin! Come on in and rest." I heard Wo's voice welcome me as I stepped in the room. I saw the left wall where Granddaddy's dresser once stood. He kept candy bars and gum in that top drawer. My cousin Lisa and I would help ourselves, especially to the chocolate.

Throughout the house I smelled food, saw the faces, heard the voices and music, felt the hugs and without a doubt I felt the love that always dwelled in that house. I remembered the talks with Wo whether she was healing a heartache or advising me how I need to *"let the Lord handle that, dahlin."*

Walking through that house the 6th chapter of Deuteronomy came to my mind. That chapter instructs Israel to teach their children (and in this case grandchildren) to never forget God. In verse five, He commands to love the Lord with all your heart, soul, strength and mind. In verse seven, He instructs them: Impress these (the commandments) on your children. Talk about them when you sit at home and when you walk along the road, when you lie down and when you get up.

In other words: *tell your children about the Lord.*

Verse 20 instructs parents on how to answer their children's questions about God. Tell them that the Lord rescued you. Every opportunity you have tell your children about the Lord. Tell how He saved you. Tell how He carried you through those times you weren't sure how you'd make it. Tell them about the Lord. Tell them as they grow up to never forget God.

There have been numerous times the past years when I've said, "I wish Wo was here and she could tell me what to do." There are plenty of things that have occurred that I'm glad she hasn't been here to see. Some things I wish she could see. I wish she could have known my brother Philip's three children. I wish she could have known my great-nieces, Mackenzie and Paisley.

Most of all, I'd want her to know that I never forgot what she taught me. The ways she encouraged me, believed in me, pampered me, spoiled me, but most of all taught me to never forget God - all the days of my life.

AUGUST - WEEK ONE

Let's Play Church — Romans 12: 1-2

Growing up with two older brothers in a preacher's family, we found quite a bit of fascination with activities that went on in church. Why wouldn't we? We never missed a service. Sunday morning, Sunday night, Wednesday night and EVERY "Gospel Meeting" in town - we knew exactly who, when, where and what went on during any service in the local Churches of Christ.

Being close in age, the three of us would end up playing together and on cold rainy days, we would find something to do inside. Many times that game would be going to the living room and playing church. Maybe we chose that game because we loved our Daddy so much and loved what he did for a living and we wanted to be just like him.

OK- you can't tell me any kid who grew up going to church didn't do the same thing. We probably had it set up just like anybody else. Gary was the song leader, Philip led the prayer and of course, no big surprise of who preached. That would be me. In fact, I wouldn't play unless I got to be the preacher. Being the preacher meant I was in charge (so I thought) and those two brothers of mine had better do things EXACTLY the way I wanted them to. Gary was suppose to lead three songs before the prayer, not two. We had communion before the sermon, not after. If they didn't play right, I wouldn't play with them.

Gary led his songs and Philip prayed...and prayed...and prayed...usually for the same sick soul every week. Our sick list never changed. After the prayer, it was then time for "the opportunity." Now, "the opportunity" was actually our interpretation of communion or The Lord's Supper. In regular worship services we would hear the grown-ups pray, "Lord, we thank you for the OPPORTUNITY..." so, we thought that's what it was called.

If Gary led "Break Thou The Bread of Life" before communion, I would yell at him, "Gary - that's not a song for the opportunity - that's a regular song." Then, I'd knock him upside the head, "PLAY RIGHT!"

If Philip prayed too long and didn't ask God to "guide, guard and direct us, I'd knock him in the head too and say, "PLAY RIGHT!"

After "the opportunity", Gary would lead us in "the stand-up song". That song is upbeat, fast, usually a "Stamps-Baxter" favorite and we'd belt it out loud as we could, and maybe sang the chorus twice. That was the song that was supposed to wake you up and get you fired up, ready to hear the sermon. That's why you didn't sing songs like "Asleep in Jesus" or "Ready To Suffer". Those really aren't the best titles to sing before the sermon.

After "the stand-up song", I would get up and start my sermon by yelling out, "... and the whole church said - Amen!" Then, I would preach the most faith-finding, soul-searching, heart rendering sermon any five year old could preach. I'd fold my

Bible in half and urge my audience "YOU BETTER BE BAB-BA-TIZED!" After a few more urgent words, I'd close my sermon with the typical, "Won't you come, as together we stand and sing".

At that time, Gary would get up and start leading us in 450 verses of "Just As I Am". Now, Philip, being the laid back easy going kid that he was, was always the sinner. Gary could have been, but he had far more to confess than Philip. Since sinners always sat in the back, Philip would sit in the bathroom so he would have a long hall to walk down to the living room. It gave him a good aisle to walk down.

By verse 350 of "Just As I Am", here came Philip down the hall/aisle. I would point back to the bathroom and say, "Not yet. Wait a few more verses." I would want Gary to sing another verse, then I would stop him and urge my audience some more and preach another 5 minute sermon in between verses.

It was around verse 375 that Philip would start back up the hall/aisle and I would stomp my foot and say, "NO! You're not playing right!" "What do you mean I'm not playing right? I waited until 20 verses?"

I would get so mad because he wasn't playing right and send him back only to have him come back after another 20 verses. Again, I'd knock him upside the head and say, "That's not right!"

"What is it now?" Poor Philip let me push him around any old way. "YOU'RE NOT CRYING! IT DOESN'T COUNT UNLESS YOU CRY! Now- go back and DON'T FORGET TO CRY. PLAY RIGHT!"

Finally, Philip would go back and after that last 450th verse of "Just As I Am", here he came- just a weeping and wailing. I'd take him by the hand and ask, "Why have you come?"

Philip would try to keep from laughing and answer, *"I have come to be bab-ba-tized."*

"No, we *bab-ba-tized* you last week. You've just said and done things and brought shame and reproach on the church this week." Gary would chime in and say, "Oh, let's bab-ba-tize him so we can sing 'Oh Happy Day'. That's my favorite." To the bathtub we would go to bab-ba-tize Philip and Gary would break out into "Oh Happy Day".

I'd come back and make a few closing announcements, then we'd sing a verse of "Take The Name of Jesus With You" and that was it. From there we went to the front porch, stood around and pretended to smoke because that's what people did after church...except the preacher. Preachers didn't smoke!

I know, that's probably exactly the same way you played church, and I'm sure you have your stories and memories of how you "played church." Here's my question: Are we still PLAYING church? Are we so caught up in the motions and the mechanics that we have forgotten what really matters and what's really important?

Has our Christianity become a child's game? Are we so caught up in pointing at everybody else, getting so angry and worrying so much because "they're not playing right," that we forget our mission and forget our purpose? Rather than focusing on the cross, we're nit-picking each other. How many souls have been brought to Christ by nit-picking? Jesus warned the Pharisees in Matthew 15 about their worship being all words and in vain. Do we need the same warning?

Let's quit playing the game and grow-up.

AUGUST - WEEK TWO

Life Can Be A Pain   *2 Corinthians 1:4*

All my life I have heard many people use the figure of speech, "the patience of Job." It doesn't take an avid church attendee to be familiar with his name but sadly, this cliche "patience of Job" is the extent of their knowledge of this man. The Bible tells us, "This man was blameless and upright, he feared God and shunned evil."

Job writes in the 14th chapter verse 1; "Man born of woman is of few days and full of trouble." In other words, sooner or later your good days are going to run out and you're going to face troubles. James reinforces this thought in the New Testament- James 1:2: "Consider it pure joy, my brothers, whenever you face trials of many kinds..." He didn't say "IF you face trials" he said "WHEN". We're either in a storm, coming out of a storm or headed in to a storm.

As depressing as that sounds, it's a sad reality. As righteous and godly as Job was he still faced incredible trials- more than any of us could imagine. Take some time and read the first couple of chapters and let it soak in. His livestock, his servants, his children and eventually, his health. While it's true that through all of these trials Job never denied God, he did, however, question why. You know what? That's OK. He never blamed God, he never denied God but yes, he did ask God why. In chapter 21 Job questions why the wicked have it so good but yet the righteous suffer?

Many times, I've reflected on some conversations I've had with various friends who are dealing with some very difficult situations. One friend is grieving the loss of a parent, another is going through a divorce. I've had a couple of conversations with a friend whose grown son died after a long battle with cancer. Dad has preached a few Sunday nights in Decatur for a congregation whose 55 year old minister died very suddenly and unexpectedly.

Yes, eventually we all face pain and just like Job, it hurts. Just like Job, it's not fair when you've done nothing to deserve it. Just like Job, we all have friends who make efforts to reason with what we're going through but nothing conclusive is reached.

One of the many things I love about the book of Job is the assurance that it is not a sin to feel pain. It's not a sin to question why you're having to endure such pain. Pain is not a desired emotion. We avoid it at all cost whether it's physical pain, emotional pain, spiritual pain - whatever. We try to avoid it in our own lives but also try to "rescue" others when they're in pain. If someone we love is in a storm or having to walk through that deep, dark valley, many of us try to deem ourselves as PROBLEM SOLVERS. Rather than share their pain, we choose to solve their problem and inundate them with answers to any questions that might cross their minds.

For many years, I have traveled across this country and spoken to hundreds of ladies groups sharing with them my thoughts on how we as Christians can reach out to those who are hurting. The average American family goes through a moderate to severe crisis every three to five years. That means in any average size church, 1/3 of your members are in crisis. Do you know who they are? What are you doing to help?

The primary point that I try to get across in this lesson is that unless pain is accepted it can't be healed. Those who are hurting aren't necessarily looking for advice or solutions or answers to questions. They just want someone to ACCEPT their pain.

With the absolute best intentions, we try to offer comfort with our words but please hear me on this: VERY FEW WORDS PROVIDE COMFORT! In fact, many of our words of comfort actually BLOCK their pain rather than ACCEPT their pain. As we hear their story and the source of their pain, we immediately feel compelled to tell our story. "I went through a divorce and let me tell you about my experience…"

"We lost a child one time and let me tell you, it was tough…"

Statements like "This is God's plan…" or "God won't give you more than you can handle…" or "it takes both rain and sunshine to make a rainbow…" come from hearts that are so loving and want so badly to take away pain. Many of us try to relate to the one in pain by saying "I know how you feel" but trust me - there is absolutely no way we could know EXACTLY how someone feels. Yes, situations are similar and yes, experiences are synonymous but yet, none are exactly alike and saying, "I know how you feel" only rejects their feelings and can many times cause guilt for feeling pain.

Unless pain is accepted it can't be healed - I write those words again. As I reflect on these conversations, I see patterns forming from each one. Each person that I've spoken with are Godly, Christian people but in their words and in the tones of their voices I hear a sense of guilt. I hear the ringing of the emotion that if I feel this way, it shows a lack of faith and trust in God. To that I offer a resounding NO! No - it is not.

A dear friend shared with me a writing that she received and I was inspired by this quote:

"Let the pain run its course," says Rob Eagar. *"As humans we are so focused on wanting to feel good all the time. Then when hurt and pain come into our lives, we do anything to get rid of it. Understand that it is going to hurt for a while. Having that realization helped me to face my pain and to be able to say, 'Okay, this is how it's going to be.'"*

Please understand me on this - I in no way intend to discourage ANYONE from trying to comfort someone who is hurting. In fact, my intention is the opposite. I truly feel as Christians we are obligated to comfort those who face trials and pain. Personally, I'm just trying to find the best way to go about it. Of course, the perfect example is Jesus and how thankful I am that we're told of a time when he attended a funeral and what was His emotion at that funeral? He wept. (John 11:35)

I don't know where you are right now - in the storm - coming out of the storm? Maybe everyday is a "chance of showers". If you are faced with pain, I'm sorry. I'm truly sorry. But, if you're hurting and your tears are soaking your pillow each and every night - it's OK to hurt. You're still God's child. He still loves you and just like Job, you'll get through it. No time limits on your pain; no schedule of how to handle it. Eventually, the sun will shine again.

Maybe you're on the other side and someone you care about is hurting…

Don't be a problem solver. *Just be there.*

I Want To Be Like Johnny — James 4:10

"Johnny couldn't count to ten." Legendary University of Alabama Coach Gene Stallings was referring to his son, John Mark - when he made the statement you could hear the grief in his voice. Grief because John Mark had passed away the previous month from heart disease. He referred to John Mark, or Johnny as he called him, several times throughout the speech I heard him give in 2008 at a fundraiser. My dear friend, Kim Davis invited me to join her and her family at their table and I wouldn't have missed it for anything.

Coach Stallings is no stranger to the state of Alabama. Between 1990-1996 he was the head football coach at The University of Alabama and probably more easily recognized than the Governor. But his son, John Mark, became just as popular with Alabama fans during those years. John Mark was born in 1962 to Coach Stallings and his wife, Ruth Ann in Tuscaloosa - their third child and only son. Four sisters, two older and two younger, Johnny was quite special to the Stallings family.

Special not just because he was the only boy, but because he was born with Downs Syndrome. Hearing the news of his condition was heartbreaking to Coach and Ruth Ann but as the years went on, they quickly learned what a joy it was to have Johnny. Many times I've heard Coach make the statement, "If the good Lord took me back and told me I could choose between a healthy strong boy or Johnny, I'd take Johnny every time. No question about it."

That's quite a statement coming from a man like Coach Stallings. He played football all the years of his youth. He was tough enough to be one of Coach Bryant's "Junction Boys" while playing at Texas A&M. He later was hand picked by Coach Bryant to be an assistant at Alabama in the early 60's. It was his dream to have a son who ran for touchdowns or threw long passes or tackled quarterbacks. Instead, his son couldn't count to ten. His son had Downs Syndrome and a heart condition that would shorten his life.

Johnny couldn't count to ten, but the lives he touched were innumerable. Everyone he met, he made them feel important. He never snubbed anybody or treated them rudely, even in a crowd. He was quick to give a hug and that smile of his just made you want to be his friend.

I learned that for myself when I was honored to be in the Stallings home. Ruth Ann and I had spoken at various ladies events together and we became friends. I had met John Mark previously at ball games and in September of '94, my good friend Marilyn Ingram and I, spent an afternoon in Tuscaloosa at their home. When John Mark walked in the house after working that morning at the Paul "Bear" Bryant Museum, he lit up the whole room with his smile. It was as if everyone there was family and he was glad to have each one in his home.

It was a great privilege to meet Coach Stallings in 1993 following Alabama's 12th National Championship

Knowing what a huge Alabama fan I am, he quickly wanted to show me the memorabilia in his room. We had a great time trying to stump each other on Alabama trivia and let me tell you, he whipped me in that game. Johnny couldn't count to ten, but he had a memory like no one I've ever known. He knew every player, the number on their jersey and the greatest plays ever played.

Johnny couldn't count to ten, and he never kept score. He was quick to forgive and never held a grudge. There's a book about the life of John Mark written by Coach Stallings entitled *Another Season*. If you haven't read it, let me recommend that you read it as soon as possible. It's a quick read and you'll enjoy every page.

In that book, Coach Stallings tells of the low times in his long career. In 1971, he was fired from Texas A&M and in 1989, the Arizona Cardinals let him go. Coach Stallings explains that the owner of the Cardinals, Bill Bidwill wasn't very kind with his words. The thought of lashing back crossed Coach Stallings' mind when Johnny innocently looked at him and said, "We still love Mr. Bidwill, don't we Pop?"

Johnny couldn't count to ten, but he lived more like Jesus than a lot of the rest of us. Jesus taught that unless you become like little children, you will not enter the kingdom of Heaven. (Matthew 18:3). As an adult, Johnny never lost that childlike heart.

Johnny couldn't count to ten, but making you happy made him happy. Seeing you smile made him smile. His happiness and his fulfillment didn't come from what you did for him, but rather what he could do for you. Did you catch that statement? Did you catch it because that's a concept I can't seem to get through my head. I guess that's the strongest lesson I learned from my mere acquaintance with Johnny. He was more interested in you and always wanted to please others. Too often I find myself pinning my fulfillment and satisfaction on other people or outside things when actually, it should come from within myself.

We put undeserved pressure on family, friends, spouses, co-workers and others to make us happy. How unfair of us to put expectations on people to fulfill us when there's no way that feat is humanly possible. Johnny seemed to understand that true joy comes when you do for others and you make them happy. It doesn't come from material things or stuff. It comes from YOURSELF.

Johnny couldn't count to ten, but he can now. He had something none of the rest of us have - a one way ticket to heaven. He's missed, and no doubt, there's an emptiness in the Stallings home that's never been there before. But the impact of John Mark Stallings remarkable 46 years on this earth will last forever.

Johnny couldn't count to ten, but the rest of us can. Maybe we're all a little too smart for our own good.

Roll Tide, Johnny.

It's A Tradition — Galatians 1:8-9

One sunny Saturday morning in October, I was driving down I-65 making my way to Birmingham to pick-up my friend Melisa, then drive on to Tuscaloosa for a football game at The University of Alabama. While drivng down the interstate, the voice belonging to my brother, Philip was clear as a bell coming through my telephone ear piece. He and his family had arrived in Auburn, Alabama the night before and were attending the game there against Arkansas. He and the kids had walked down to "Tiger Rags" and bought their traditional t-shirt and other items for the game.

"What time does your game start?" I knew by them being up and going so early they probably had the morning kick-off. Not my favorite time for a football game but these universities like to get that TV money.

"We've got the 11:30 kick-off. Hopefully, that'll make it easier to get home at a decent hour." Philip was anticipating the traffic and everything else involved when 86,000 are gathered in one place.

Our conversation continued as we analyzed each game through out the Southeastern Conference for that day. We're such experts when it comes to each team's strengths and weaknesses (I hope you detected the tongue in cheek tone in that statement) and we always enjoy making our predictions of the outcomes. "If Auburn doesn't get a running game going, it's going to be a long day." "If Alabama doesn't find a way to convert those third downs and control the line of scrimmage, it won't be pretty." Like I said, real experts.

We finished our conversation about the time I was making the turn at the Hoover exit for Melisa's house. "Y'all be careful. We'll talk soon." A stop at Starbuck's for Melisa's Pumpkin Spice Latte, then on to her house to load up our tailgating gear.

As traffic picked-up on I-65, a visual came to mind and one I think would be an outstanding idea for an artist to capture. If I could paint, I think I'd name this painting, "Football Saturdays In The South". In the background, I'd have the autumn colored trees and clear blue sky with the sun shining bright. I'd paint the I-65/459 interchange in Birmingham portraying the heavy traffic of cars headed in various directions.

The vehicles on this interchange would have a variety of decorations showing allegiance to teams throughout the south. A couple of cars are headed west on 459 with flags from the University of Alabama. Some are headed east with Auburn flags. I'd include a car or two turning at the sign reading "Atlanta" and their flags are from the University of Georgia. In the upper right corner going toward the Tennessee line would be some trucks covered in orange obviously bound for Knoxville to see the Vols play.

Football in the south- it's a tradition. Since I was a small child, it's been a way of life at our house. If I'm not attending a game, I'm planted in front of the TV from the time ESPN starts at 9:00 and shut it off at midnight.

You have to understand, once that first game kicks-off Labor Day weekend, lives are planned around the football schedule. A bride will look at the schedule before she looks at a calendar to book that wedding. My mother's obstetrician teased me for years for being born just as Alabama was about to kick-off against Georgia and ruining his radio time.

Each football fan is very passionate about team traditions. Do I dare use the word "sacred" traditions? The checkered board endzone at The University of Tennessee. The fans barking as the ball is kicked-off at Georgia. I've seen "The Grove" in Oxford, Mississippi and I've got to admit, it's a thing of beauty, especially when you throw in the smell of barbecue that's been simmering all day long.

As an Alabama fan, The Quad is a tradition we enjoy. My friends, Jimmy, Randy, Lois, Melisa and I will stroll through the area where thousands have gathered to eat, play and mostly, just fellowship. The Million Dollar Band parades down the street and leads the traditional "elephant stomp" as fans make their way to Bryant-Denny Stadium with over 100,000 eager to see another game.

Tradition! You don't mess with it. You don't make fun of it or, in some places, you'll get hurt. What's a tradition in one stadium wouldn't be allowed in other stadiums. You're not going to hear cowbells in Baton Rouge like you do in Starkville, Mississippi. You're not going to see an eagle fly over the stadium in Lexington, Kentucky like you do in Auburn, Alabama. 90,000 people aren't going to stand up chopping their arms to the soundtrack from "Jaws" in Columbia, South Carolina like they do in Gainesville, Florida. What's right for one place is not right for another.

While each team has its own tradition, EVERY team has the same rule book. There are thousands of traditions out there but only one rule book. Sadly, some of our teams seem to neglect reading that rule book very closely and the consequences are tough to pay.

As fans, we are to distinguish what is tradition and what is by the rule book. The same can be said with our Christianity today. There are many things that we do in our churches that are tradition but there are many things we each should be doing that is by the "rule book", which of course, is the Bible.

It is imperative that we as Christians come to a strong understanding that the Bible, and only the Bible, is the only rule book that should be followed. Traditions are special to us and hold a special place in our hearts; however, we need to be careful when we bind those traditions on others. In churches and other religious groups there are traditions that are sometimes mistaken for doctrine.

What's right for one group might not be conducive for another, unless it's part of the rule book. Along with traditions, cultures can come into play. Dad has shared with me some of the ways they express their worship in Cuba or other countries and while it's different than how we do things in the states, it is still in compliance with God's Word. In my years of hearing my Dad preach I've heard him put it this way:

In matters of doctrine - **UNITY**
In matters of opinion - **LIBERTY**
in ALL matters - **LOVE!**

May we all love one another as God first loved us.

AUGUST - WEEK FIVE

Get Your Six Iron Out   I Peter 4:9-10

I'm not a good golfer, but I do love to play with Dad, mostly because he lets me cheat. He calls it "PGA Rules" which means "Preacher's Golf Association". It's not very blatant but every now and then if you need a little help in improving where the ball lands, use that handy club known as "the foot wedge". Mostly, our philosophy in our game is "hit it until it feels good." That means when you're at the tee box, keep driving until your ball lands where you it want to be.

After spending some time with the family on Labor Day, Dad and I sneaked off and played nine holes before the sun went down. The little course we play in Arab is not as difficult as others, but it has a few challenges here and there- especially for me who is challenged at Putt Putt. One particular hole, I had a great drive off the tee box. I do that occasionally and that's usually when I take a picture to savor the moment. I bet it went well over 200 yards and landed right in the middle of the fairway, which for me, is rare. I had another 100 yards to the green, but there was a problem. A good size pond of water was between my ball and the green. The only way to the green was over the water. Any other hole, I could just pull out my five iron and hit to the green. That water hazard glared me in the face.

It was a mental thing. Just hit over it, but I couldn't shake that possibility of shanking it and SPLASH! I didn't have to play golf for very long before I learned that those silly little balls don't float. I tried to block it from my mind and look directly at the green. I tried to remember great advice from Ty Webb (played by Chevy Chase) in the movie "Caddyshack". "Be the ball. Be the ball. Just BE the ball." I got a focal point right in the middle of the green and never looked at that hazard in front of me.

The club came out of my bag and I made my approach. The video played in my mind of the ball sailing in the air and landing right in the middle of the green, leaving with me about a 3 feet putt. I was ready. My head was down and my left arm was straight. The club came back and right in the middle of my back swing the thought swooshed through my head, "DON'T HIT THE WATER!" While hitting a golf ball, one of the keys is to keep your head down. Raising up while swinging guarantees failure. If you want to see a bad shot, just look up.

Well, that's exactly what I did and SPLASH! That Maxfli sank faster than a rock. I could almost hear the fish giggling at the bottom of that pond and a turtle sitting on the bank just shaking his head. *"You raised up, Cindi!"*

Dad is always so kind when I make a shot like that. To myself I was thinking, "Nice shot, Shank-a-potamus!" I put the club back in the bag and told Dad that I would just drop on the other side of the pond. I started walking toward the cart when he just stood there looking at me.

Dad said, "No! Get a ball and hit again." I didn't want to lose another ball, but he said, "You won't if you'll hit with the right club. Get your six iron and hit it again."

I really didn't want to. I was running low on golf balls and they're not cheap. But, since Dad insisted, I did as he said. "I really don't want to. I'll just hit another one in the water."

"No you won't, if you'll use the right club". He continued giving me instructions as I pulled out the six iron and put a little more thought into my shot. "Keep your head down and don't pull back so far in your swing." I approached the ball and he said, "Open the face of the club a little more to get some loft on it." His voice sounded so determined but also spoke with a lot of confidence. "Now, take that six iron and place that ball right on the green."

I followed Dad's instructions. Head down, left arm straight and not pulling the club back to far. The swing felt good and made that "swoosh" sound as I hit the sweet spot of the ball. The ball sailed through the air and BINGO! Right on the green! I had about a four foot putt to the hole and since we cheat, we counted it as a birdie - three strokes on a par 4.

WOO HOO! I DID IT! I pulled out that six iron, got over that water hazard and landed right on the green. One of my finer moments in golf. I don't even remember what I scored that day, but I clearly remember that hole that I birdied because I took out my six iron.

Getting through this life can be very discouraging. Plans can be made and schedules set and then, there it is. How can I ever get over this hurdle? The college student well on his way to getting that degree and then he learns they added calculus to his curriculum. He's terrible at math and needed a tutor to get through high school algebra. How will he ever overcome this one?

There's a young wife raising two children, trying to educate them, keep them safe and teach them the ways of the Lord and how to be Christian godly people. Just as the younger of the two starts to kindergarten her husband decides he wants out and would rather live with someone else, leaving her with two children all alone. How will she ever get those children raised all by herself?

That's when we need someone to tell us "You can do this. Get your six iron out!" With determination, confidence and focus, any hazard can be overcome. Paul's "six iron" was found in Philippians 4:13 where he wrote, "I can do ALL things through Christ who strengthens me."

The book of Acts records the actions of the early church and how the gospel spread throughout the region. One of the men who played a vital part in the early church was Barnabas. You don't read of him being an outstanding preacher. He didn't blow anyone away with his speaking skills nor was he one to set up all the Bible studies with others. His gift was the gift of encouraging. Barnabas was an encourager. He was the one who encouraged Paul and so many others and kept things positive.

Who is the Barnabas in your life? Or, a better question, are YOU someone's Barnabas? When you're ready to quit, who tells you, "Don't give up. Don't quit! Don't let Satan have the advantage."

I want to be like Barnabas. I want to hold the hand of others and remind them to stand strong. That's what Barnabas did, and he was good at it.

Life is full of hazards. Get your six iron out!

SEPTEMBER - WEEK ONE

Write Your Own Dash — James 4:13

If you've ever walked through a cemetery, you see rows and rows of headstones of the deceased. Most of them display the name of the deceased, their date of birth and their date of death. For example the headstone of Elvis Presley reads: **ELVIS AARON PRESLEY, JANUARY 8, 1935 - AUGUST 16, 1977**. As far as a headstone goes, your life is simply when you're born and when you died. You live - you die! That's it.

There's something else included in those dates besides the month, day and year of both events. I had never really put much thought in to it but lately, I've noticed it a lot more. It's the dash mark. That small, little line between the date of birth and the date of death. A dash. James writes in chapter 4, verse 13 about (I'm paraphrasing here) how we make all kinds of plans and visions for our lives. Then he writes beginning in verse 14, through inspiration of the Holy Spirit: What is your life? You are a mist that appears for a little while and then vanishes.

I translate James by saying, "Your life is a dash. It's just a line between your date of birth and your date of death. None of us have any idea just how long that line will be so, we should live in God's will, make the most of every day and realize, He's the one in charge."

We have in our minds that our dash will last a long, long time. One evening I read that the oldest person alive in 2009 passed away at age 115. One hundred and fifteen years! WOW! That's a long time. Born in 1894 and lived through all of the amazing events of the 20th century - World War I, the Great Depression, the attack on Pearl Harbor, World War II, the invention of the television and all of the amazing advances in technology. What a long time to live.

On the other hand, some dashes are just far too short and they come to an end far too quickly. We don't see it coming. One day a loved one is right with us and the next day, family and friends are gathered in an overflow room of the Emergency Room crying and comforting each other. I wish I had kept a record of the ages of patients who passed away during my time when I worked in the Emergency Room at Huntsville Hospital. There were plenty who were quite elderly and had lived long lives but I truly believe the patients 65 and younger far out numbered them.

Tuesday, September 8, 2009 was one of THOSE days. I returned from lunch planning to make routine visits in patient rooms of the hospital when my phone rang. My dear friend, Pat Roberson asked me to please go to the ER because her son-in-law had passed out in the yard and was on his way via ambulance. A co-worker, Cheryl Davis, who is a good friend of the families ran with me across the street. Within a few minutes, the news was not good.

Tim Nash was in full arrest when the ambulance arrived. The doctor and staff did everything humanly possible, giving medications, injections and even shocking his heart - but to no avail. Around 1:30 that afternoon, Tim was pronounced dead.

Thirty-one years old. A husband, A father. A son. A brother. A deacon. A tireless servant of the Lord. An engineer. A Bible class teacher. A friend. Trying to maintain some type of professionalism as a hospital employee, I eventually broke down sobbing in the corner, begging God to just make this bad dream go away. This couldn't be happening.

Every Sunday, Tim sat in the pew just behind me with his wife, Kacey and two precious daughters, along with Kacey's parents. He was quiet,but so focused on being a good husband and being a good Dad. A man this good with a family this good is not suppose to die at 31 years of age. He's suppose to grow old with his wife who loves him more than life itself and watch his little girls grow up. It made no sense. Calli had just turned 4 a few days before and Betsy had her 2nd birthday in August. How in the world would they process the fact that Daddy wasn't coming home that night?

It still makes no sense. But, who says it has to make sense? The only conclusion that I come to is this: As a human being, I had no control over what day I was born nor will I have any control over what day I leave this earth. My sovereign Holy Father in heaven holds that control. I have no say in just how long that dash is.

I do, however, have a say in the contents of that dash. If you could break open the dash and see what's inside, what would you find? Would you find a person who was loving and kind to others? Would you find a person who cherished his/her family? Would you find a person who made life better for those they came in contact with? Would you find a person who strives each and every day to live for God and become more like Christ every day?

I have resolved to honestly approach each new day as a gift. The slate is clean and I've been given a brand new start. It's another day to strengthen my dash and try as best I can to fill it with God's will and plan.

Life is just a dash. What's in yours?

Tim's short life left an eternal legacy of family and faith we will never forget

Heroes — Exodus 13:3-16

The trip of a lifetime came for me in March of 2009. For years, my good friend, Karen Brunner and I talked about how much fun it would be to travel to New York City. Karen lives in Richmond, VA and getting together doesn't happen real often for us. That's why I was blown away when Karen's husband, Scott, contacted me and said he wanted to surprise Karen with a trip to The Big Apple.

Scott made the arrangements and informed Karen of his incredibly kind gesture. Karen immediately phoned me and we squealed and shared our "giddiness" like we were still teenagers. Karen and I have been friends since she was 15 years old and we remained friends through college years, early adulthood and now here we are all grown up. In fact, I was the one who suggested to Scott, "You ought to ask out Karen Pate. I think y'all would be a good fit." He did and in 1991 he married her. One of the most meaningful honors of my life was when she asked me to be her maid of honor and I stood by her as she said those wedding vows to Scott.

There we were, two life long friends beginning our adventure in New York. Karen had everything mapped out perfectly. New York is not foreign territory to her so she knew exactly what sights to see, how to get there and the best time to visit.

I knew I wanted to go to the top of the Empire State Building, see the Statue of Liberty, Rockefeller Plaza, Times Square at night, Central Park, China Town and Wall Street; however, the absolute number one attraction that I did not want to miss was a few blocks from Wall Street. From the very minute Scott told me of this trip, seeing this attraction was the first thing that popped in my mind.

After seeing the Statue of Liberty, a subway ride took us to the financial district - Wall Street. I got a great view of the New York Stock Exchange building as well as City Hall. From there, just a few blocks away- my heart fluttered. For about 7 1/2 years, I had longed to see Ground Zero. The sight where the World Trade Centers once stood until that horrific day on September 11, 2001.

Karen pointed out where Rudy Guliani ran from City Hall immediately after receiving word. Everything else, I could piece together myself as I remembered being glued to the TV through that horrible day and many days following. Construction was going on during our time there, so our view was obstructed. That was OK. I felt a little embarrassed as I approached the area with eyes full of tears. I felt like the typical tourist as I photographed every inch of the area.

I then became aware of my surroundings and experienced something that had not occurred at the other attractions we visited. "Listen!" I whispered to Karen as we stepped toward the barricades. "Listen at how quiet it is." It was an immediate sense of reverence. There were no signs that read "QUIET PLEASE", nor was there a guard or officer instructing guests to be respectful. It came natural for anyone in the area. I didn't want to hum out loud, but in my head I was hearing,

"We are standing on Holy Ground and I know that there are angels all around..."

Directly across the street is the fire station, within a stone's throw of the towers. The firefighters at this station were the first to respond on that horrific day. Many lost their lives trying to rescue the victims. Nothing elaborate about this station. They didn't replace the floors with marble or build fancy tall columns in the front.

I looked down the street and visually remembered watching on TV the people running as the towers fell and the smoke, dust and debris covered the area. The ferry boat that Karen and I had just ridden from Ellis Island was used on that day to evacuate people.

Walking in front of that fire station I saw the plaques and tributes. Visitors continued to leave flowers, pictures of loved ones and memorabilia. I'm not sure anything that I have ever seen as a tourist has touched my heart more than Ground Zero. My hands touched the wall that contain the sculptures of firefighters and first responders. No second guessing; no hesitation; these heroes sacrificed their own lives to save others. Through my mind, I continued to remember that I was on the ground where people had sacrificed their own lives for someone else. My embarrassment eased when I saw another lady wiping her eyes as she looked at the wall just as I tried to hide my emotion. These men and women were somebody's husband, somebody's wife, somebody's dad, somebody's sister; EVERYBODY'S HERO!

All over the area, there were several signs that read, "We Will Never Forget! September 11, 2001!" Of course, I haven't forgotten, but how easily I've forgotten the faces of the ones who lost their lives. I had not thought about the sacrifices that were made and how some risked their own lives to save another. Seeing the actual sight brought it back to the surface. It made me thankful again for those who are willing to put their lives on the line, just so the rest of us can be safe.

God has always wanted His people to remember. I think He knew we would become distracted and forget. People all over the world recognize the name of Jesus and show some sort of respect and reverence toward Him. But, do we truly see Him as the one who gave His life so we could be free from Satan's bondage?

As Christians, we have our own memorial. A feast that I am blessed to participate in every Sunday because it's so easy for me to forget and I often need to be reminded of the sacrifice made by my Lord and Savior Jesus Christ. This memorial is not a fancy building. It's not a huge statue and it's not even a plaque. It's much more simple than that. It's a piece of unleaven bread, usually a wafer or cracker that represents the broken body of Christ. It's also a cup of grape juice which represents the blood of my Savior that He shed for me.

Seeing the pictures of the men and women who died for others is moving and something I will NEVER forget. Someone died so others can live. Someone also died so ALL can live. His name is Jesus. May we never forget.

SEPTEMBER - WEEK THREE

Why Aren't You Married? *I Corinthians 7:1*

The gathering was set for right after evening services on a Sunday night. When you are a member of a congregation that has 500 or more members, being in a small group makes it so much easier to get closer to other members and make a connection. Our group was always full of life where we shared lots of laughs as well as attempting to lighten any burdens that might come around.

I was informed of the menu: Ham (bought by the hosts), potato salad, baked beans, green salad, rolls, cakes, pies, cookies, tea and coffee. Reading that list, I informed the hostess I would be glad to make baked beans and a chess pie. Here's the response she sent:

"Cindi, being a single girl I know you don't spend much time in the kitchen. Why don't you just bring some bags of ice."

ICE? Are you sure? Have you got a recipe for that? Did you want crushed, cubed, shaved, pebbled or what? Was that with a lemon twist or lime slice? Yes, the sarcasm ran through my head but I kept it to myself. I was only 28 years old and at the time I knew I was no Paula Deen. My Mother won the Home Economics award in high school but, I didn't even take Home Ec. But, I still knew my way around the kitchen well enough to make some basic items. Others had even complimented my baked beans and asked for a recipe. There's just something magical about a wedding band that makes you a good cook.

I'm all for marriage. I think it's a great idea. One of my claims to fame is that I've been a bridesmaid 17 times. You read that correctly, SEVENTEEN! OK - I'm counting the time I was four and a flower girl. I vaguely remember the green velvet dress I had to wear and carrying a white wicker basket filled with rose petals. Word has it that I walked down the aisle just prior to the bride's arrival, held up my basket and poured all of the contents right in the floor. From there, I walked over and stood by my Daddy.

I was always thrilled when one of my friends would ask me to be part of absolutely the most important day of her life. I have great memories of some fun times we had in the planning, showers, bachelorette trips to the beach, rehearsals and then the wedding. I'd be remiss if I didn't add that some of those bridesmaid dresses were... how can I say it...challenging to any sense of fashion I might have, but, I should allow some serious slack here because most occurred in the 1980's. Those puffy "Lady Di" sleeves were a must, as well as colors like mauve, aubergine and peach - which on me was a tacky orange.

There were lots of those weddings that were just flat out fun. My dear friends, Buddy and Stephanie Bell were married in 1984 and I was thrilled to be one of their bridesmaids. I'd have to say that wedding stands out as the "funnest" ones I've been in. There has been no greater honor bestowed upon me by a friend than when my dear, "close as a sister" friend, Karen Brunner asked me to be her maid of honor. It is still a thrill that I carry in my heart 20 years later. She actually asked ME to stand beside her as she said those vows to Scott.

I've seen it all in weddings- crying grooms, brides that should have made a run for it BEFORE the wedding, children wetting their pants while standing in front of 400 people, groomsmen fainting, preachers saying the wrong names...you name it - I've seen it.

Being 50 years old, the question is often posed to me, "Cindi, why aren't you married?" and I've never known how to answer that. I've come up with some creative responses:

Well, the fellow I have in mind hasn't made parole so we're waiting a while." "We talk about it often but anytime we bring it up it makes his wife so mad so we drop it."

"Why? And have to share my millions?" "I'm trying to talk him out of the priesthood and it's a challenge."

No, this isn't how I actually respond but sometimes it would fun to see what kind of reaction I'd get. Maybe being married is something God knew I would not be good at, so he chose not to put me there. Maybe the right man just hasn't come along. Maybe I'm not the right one for the ones who have come along. Only the good Lord himself knows the answer to those questions.

I am, however, very thankful that marriage is not a requirement for salvation. Yes, there are times when my life would be much easier if I weren't alone. Yes, it does get old going to movies, ball games, parties or other events by myself. It's not fun to be considered "half a person" if you don't have another half with you.

I guess there are times in our lives when we want what we don't have. If we live in the mountains, we want to live at the beach. If we're at the beach, we want to live by the lake. If we live in the city, we want to be in the country. If we have a red car, we want the blue car. If we have a dog, we want a cat. If we have three children, we want four...well, wait a minute on that one.

One of the saddest statements I hear from married people is, "Cindi, be glad you're single. Don't make the same mistake I did." That breaks my heart.

The Apostle Paul wrote a great deal about joy and contentment throughout the book of Philippians. In the fourth chapter, he tells us how he learned to be content, no matter what state he was in. He's been full and he's been hungry. He's had plenty and he has been in need. He throws in how he maintains that characteristic of contentment when he writes in verse 13, "I can do all things through Christ who strengthens me."

Are you there yet with your contentment? I didn't ask if you were happy, I asked if you were content. Are you accepting the things that you can't change and making the adjustments for your life? Have you surrendered to the fact that God knows what's best and He will supply whatever I need - not always what I want. (Philippians 4:19) I think my friend, Sisty, puts Paul's teachings into these words: "If we could all go to bed grateful and wake up thankful, life would be a lot easier."

If being single is God's plan for me, then so be it. I'll go solo to the movies. I'll keep doing ALL the chores myself around the house. I'll keep bringing "just ICE" to the parties. After all, God's just trying to get me home.

SEPTEMBER - WEEK FOUR

What Are You Wearing? *Micah* 7:19

I have spent quite a bit of time studying the life of David. Without a doubt, he is my favorite and I love to read the stories throughout the books of First and Second Samuel. I've been honored to teach classes on Sunday morning and Wednesday night at Mayfair and the life of David has been the focus of study many times.

David is such an incredible icon throughout the entire Bible. He was handsome, brave and known as "the man after God's own heart" (Acts 13:22). He's mentioned more in the New Testament than any other person from the Old Testament. When people are asked to name their favorite person in the Bible, many times David is chosen. Even Hollywood has portrayed David in various films and story lines.

The Bible doesn't "sugar coat" the story of our heroes. The Holy Spirit guided its writers to include the bad along with the good. We get the complete story and for that I'm thankful. He was a human being with weakness just like the rest of us. What fascinates me about the account of David's fall in II Samuel 11 is the brevity of the scriptures. Not a lot of details are written but enough for us to clearly understand what transpired during those days.

While studying the lessons taught from David's sin with Bathsheba, one of the 7th graders in my class made an interesting observation. I love the way these girls think because it's so innocent and so real. She said, "You know, David should have just confessed everything right after he sinned with Bathsheba because everybody was going to find out about it anyway. It's all written in the Bible." In other words, why try to hide it because we're all going to read about it eventually.

She was right. The embarrassment and detail of David's mistakes are right there in print. Not only David but many others throughout the Bible. It makes me very thankful that my sins aren't recorded for all the world to see.

When I read of men like David and others whose sins are exposed, I should never feel self-righteous or compare my life to theirs. I need Jesus and His forgiveness just as much as the adulterous woman in John 8, the woman at the well in John 4 or the thief on the cross in Luke 23. I may not be guilty of the same sins as they, but my need for forgiveness is just as strong.

That's why I'm thankful to be clothed in Jesus.

I once saw a special on the Discovery Channel featuring baby lambs being born. Obviously, it wasn't football season and the Braves weren't on when I landed on this channel. During the birth process, a baby lamb died and the ewe grieved her loss. Another ewe gave birth, but this ewe died in the process. So, in order for the orphaned lamb to survive the shepherds took it to the ewe who lost her lamb to let it nurse. The ewe smelled the orphaned lamb all over its body and kicked it away. It wasn't hers. The shepherds sheered the hide from the lamb that died and placed it on the orphaned lamb.
Again, the ewe smelled the orphaned lamb and let it nurse. It was clothed in her baby's hide, so it was hers.
That's what God did for us. When we were buried in baptism we were clothed in Christ and received a robe of forgiveness. Just like the rebellious son in Luke 15, God robes us with forgiveness. Even more, what's under your robe is strictly between you and God. It's nobody else's business. Only God knows and only God can forgive.

That robe is mine not because I'm so good, but because God is good.

I didn't earn it - and couldn't have earned it, even if I tried.

So the same God who forgave

- David

- The woman at the well

- The adulterous woman

- and all the others... He forgives me, too...

...every day.

OCTOBER - WEEK ONE

When The Doctor Is The Patient — *Hebrews 4:15*

It was noisy around the desk area as doctors, nurses and techs reviewed charts, checked schedules and prepared for a full day of surgeries. Preparations get going around 5am for the first surgery at 7:30. It's all got to be in order before an operation can take place.

I was new to the department so there were still many new faces, especially with the anesthesiologists and surgeons. I don't see them day in and day out like I do the nurses so it is difficult to keep up with faces and names. Dr. Foster (not his real name) stepped to the desk and everyone in the room applauded. He blushed and even got a little misty eyed. Some hugged his neck, others shook his hand and everyone was so pleased to see him.

"Welcome back, Doc! You're looking good." "We missed you. How are you feeling? Any more treatments?"

He answered the questions with a smile and said many times over,

"It's good to be back. I missed all of you as well. It's no fun being the patient. This ordeal has been a much better education for me as a doctor than medical school ever was."

Isn't that interesting? A doctor now knows how it feels. He found out what it's like to occupy the bed as opposed to standing by the bed. Rather than reading the chart, it was his health information that filled the chart. Instead of the patient, a doctor has to put on that gown that has no backside. I told a patient one time who was wearing a hospital gown, "That's why we call it I C U."

As a patient, this doctor had to sit in the waiting room for a 9:00 appointment but the clock now reads 11:50 and it's not looking good for his name to be called anytime soon. Those six month old magazines got stale after the first hour. He now knows how it feels to be told not to eat or drink anything prior to the tests that were supposed to be completed long before lunch time.

What has been a routine, day in and day out for this doctor for over 25 years, is now brand new territory. Normal daily activities and protocols aren't quite as clear now that he's on this side of the waiting area. Is it really a "simple procedure" when it's inflicted in your body? No reason to be concerned or scared.

"Your doctor will phone you with the results as soon as we get them from the lab."

He's now the one sitting by the phone wondering if it will ring. He's the one who finally breaks down and calls his doctor only to hear the nurse say, as papers are rustling in the background:

Well, I'm not sure those results have come back...no wait that's Fossler not Foster...let me see...

I'll have to call you back."

When the call came, he was told,

"Well, we found something and I need you to come in and let's talk - how about next Tuesday afternoon?"

That's when he's on the side of waiting...and wondering...and worrying...and speculating...and waiting some more...

Dr. Foster told us the morning of his return, every med student should be a "mock" patient sometime and see how it feels. There are things that doctors, nurses and other medical personnel see every day and become immune to them, but to a patient, there's fear, there's anticipation, there's fatigue...it's life changing.

Having been through the crisis of a serious illness and the roller coaster of emotions, Dr. Foster will relate to his patients far better than any doctor in that hospital. He will think twice before he keeps his patients waiting without being informed as to why. He will be much more prone to provide comfort as he relays bad news, rather than just giving information.

Jesus is the Great Physician. He is the Comforter. When I hurt, He hurts. He sees my tears and my pain is in His heart. That's the true meaning of compassion - your pain in my heart. Throughout the four gospels we come across the statement:

"and Jesus had compassion upon them..."

Jesus has compassion on you, too. Isn't it amazing that God, in His infinite wisdom sent His son to live among us (Philippians 2)? He faced temptations like we do. He was rejected even in His own home town. His own family didn't have anything to do with Him for a while. He knew pain - physical and emotional pain.

But, He remained perfect. There was absolutely no guilt in His life, but He was more than willing to take on my guilt - even to the point of dying on a cruel cross.

I like knowing there are doctors out there who know how it feels to be a patient.

That's the kind of doctor I want to treat me and my family.

I like knowing I have a Savior who knows how it feels to live on this earth...

That's the kind of Savior I want to serve *forever*.

OCTOBER - WEEK TWO

Please Carry Me *Jeremiah 18:6*

    I had an appointment the other day at an office close to Huntsville Hospital. Obviously, many physicians have their offices in that area and it's a busy part of town. Walking to my car, something caught my attention. I didn't want to be impolite and stare so I tried to be subtle.

    A car pulled up at the door to the awning of an office building. A nurse wheeled a male patient toward the car and positioned the wheel chair next to the passenger side. The driver of the car stepped out and took over as the nurse locked the wheels of the chair and offered her assistance in transferring the patient to the vehicle.

    The patient was completely helpless. He was an older gentleman who was unable to move his arms and legs. His demeanor was pleasant but he also looked humble as he faced those who were assisting him. The driver of the car looked to be younger but favored the man, so it was easy for me to assume it was his son. The son placed his arms around his father and picked him up as if he were a small child. He then pulled his dad's limp body toward him and "swung" him to the passenger seat of the car. The father's body was totally limp as he fell into the seat. The son picked up his legs and placed them in front of his dad's body. He buckled his seatbelt, straightened his Bama cap that was on his head, closed the door and walked to his side of the car. He thanked the nurse and she returned inside the office.

    My witnessing of this ended, but in my mind the picture was clear. It was a safe assumption that the son would take his father home, pull into the driveway and go through the same routine. While the rest of us are able to maneuver our own bodies in and out of a vehicle, this son would again have to physically carry his dad into the house.

    Someone, whether it be this son or another caregiver would have to feed this man, bathe him and put him to bed. Normal routine activities that we do every day are not possible for this man because of his disability. He is totally dependent on someone else for things we don't even think about as we do them.

    As I remember seeing this in front of that office building, I recall the dad's eyes as he looked at his son. I'm not sure if the dad could speak or not because I never heard him say anything. His eyes said it all. His eyes said:

"Son, it's all up to you. I'm in your arms and your care."

    There have been times in my life when I've been accused of being stubborn. I feel like I can be pretty easy going, but every now and then I hear, "Cindi Bradley you are sooooooooo stubborn!" Maybe I am. Writing this, I've tried to come up with a specific example of my stubborness but I'm at a loss. Maybe I should hand the keyboard over to my friend, Sisty, and she'd come up with quite a list of the times I've been stubborn. Perhaps that's part of the weakness - not being able to site those times of my obstinate ways.

But, when it comes to doing the will of God, I want Him to disable my stubbornness. I want Him to paralyze me. He loves me too much to make me a robot. He's not going to take away my talents (as limited as they are) or my abilities.

He's not going to take away my options to choose as He wants me to surrender. But, I want Him to make me and mold me as a potter molds the clay into the shape He desires. Don't break my spirit but break my will. Break my stubbornness. Not Cindi's way- GOD'S WAY.

That dad's dependence was obvious as he looked at his son with eyes of trust. He knew there was no one else who would care for him so tenderly. That nurse cared about him, but only that son had a deep, unconditional and undying love for his Dad.

I want to have the same look of trust and dependency as I look at God's Son. He, too has that deep, unconditional and undying love for me. It was enough to carry Him to the cross...

... all for me.

Philip and me in 1963. My brother pulled me in that wagon many times. If I needed him to, he would carry me.

OCTOBER - WEEK THREE

Cave Dwellers   *Galatians 6:10*

In I Samuel 17, we read one of the most famous stories in the Bible. People who did not grow up going to church know the story of David and Goliath. Many in the world of sports use this story to illustrate their team playing a stronger team and some how overcoming any weaknesses and coming out with a victory.

What an act of heroics. I bet we all grew up with a bully in our class, probably third or fourth grade. There was the kid who ate the paste. The kid who mixed up all the items on his lunch tray and ate it. The nerdy kid who messed up your grade if there was a curve. Then there was the bully. You know, the kid in the class that was bigger than everybody else probably because he was held back in kindergarten and/or first grade. He thrived on picking on the other kids. He never had any true friends, but rather kids who were too scared not to play with him. He was all about intimidation.

That was Goliath. He stood over nine feet tall and his mouth was three times bigger than that. The Bible describes him as "The Champion" of the Philistines and yes, he was very obnoxious with his title. Each day he would yell out to the children of Israel, "SEND SOMEONE TO FIGHT ME." His taunting went on for days and his intimidation was successful as the Israelites would hide in fear.

Finally, it was David who rose up and I bet you know the story. With one stone from that sling shot, the giant fell. Just for safe measure, he decapitated Goliath and that big bully with the mouth was dead. The Champion was taken down by a young, wimpy kid who played in the band.

David was the greatest. He was the most popular guy in the land and he was hailed by all as the hero. If he was like any other 17 year old in our day, he was top dude on campus. He would have had no problem getting a date to the Homecoming Dance. In fact, the entire football team would have changed their mascot to "Giant Slayer!"

But, life didn't stay on easy street very long for David. Five chapters later, David is at one of the lowest points in his life and even fleeing for his life. Saul was obsessed with killing David causing him to leave his own country. In I Samuel 22, we find David all alone in a cave; a dark, secluded, lonely cave. His wife couldn't help him. He and his best friend Jonathan, Saul's son, had to part ways. His mentor, Samuel, had to go a different direction. David even had to stoop so low as to act like a crazy man in order to survive spending a few days with the Philistines.

David in a cave! The one who became "the man after God's own heart." The one who, as an adolescent teen, was anointed by God's man to one day be a king. Previously, the people of Israel cheered David singing, "Saul killed his thousands, David his ten thousands." From the top of the mountain to the lowest of lows, David finds himself sorting through it all in a cave!

I'm not a big fan of caves. Living close to the mountains, there are tourist attractions that will take you into caves, but you won't find me buying a ticket. There are even people out there known as "spelunkers" who explore caves and stay in there for days. Not me. I remember the Andy Griffith episode when Andy and Helen explored a cave and got trapped. Of course they escaped, but it was ol' Barney that got credit for the heroic rescue.

Have you ever felt like you were in a cave emotionally? The feeling that you're all alone and there is no way to meet the demands required of you.

You're on the run as the enemy chases you, demanding your soul. If he can convince you to buy his lies, you're as good as dead spiritually. Maybe I can relate to David in some way as he was forced to retreat to this cave. Personally, I prefer my beach chair planted in fluffy white sand at the shore rather than a dark, cold, wet cave. There are those times when you just need to be by yourself, escape from the enemy and sort through emotions. My beach chair becomes a sweet solace for me. Many decisions have been made in that chair, as well as chapters for this book written and maybe a broken heart mended. I've sat there by myself and I've sat there with great friends like Melisa, Sisty, Laura, Mary or Regina.

How do we spend our time when we retreat to the cave? Do we turn to God? Do we turn to His people? Or, do we throw the world's biggest pity party? Do I build up a false sense of independence telling myself, "I can handle this alone?"

Or, do I realize how absolutely, totally and completely dependent I am on God and there is no way to defeat my enemy, known as Satan, alone. Are you curious as to how David spent his time in this cave? Read the 57th Psalm. He cried. He prayed. He wrote psalms. He begged the Lord for mercy. He leaned on the Lord.

Do I allow others to encourage me? Eventually, David's father and brothers got word of his location and joined him in the cave. Some of the people of Israel felt David's pain as they too, were oppressed and suffering from Saul's reign as king. Like David, they became cave dwellers. It's your first biblical example of a support group. First from God, then his family and extended family, David finds the comfort he needs and rises as a leader.

There will be days you'll spend in the cave. For various reasons, Satan will force you to escape...

...whom will you allow to join you?

Melisa and Sisty - my fellow "cave dwellers"

OCTOBER - WEEK FOUR

"I'm 'Dopted"   Ephesians 1:5

My friend, Anna Dreyfuss, with her adorable Ethiopian son, Coooper

My two brothers made life a little tough for me growing up. Being the only girl and the baby, they made sure I stayed very humble. Annoying me, and on several occasions scaring me, was their favorite past time. Mother had a huge cedar chest that stored keepsakes and various items for her. Outfits that we wore home from the hospital when we were born were in there and perhaps her wedding dress and things like that. Philip found it amusing to hide in that chest and reenact something creepy from the afternoon television show "Dark Shadows." That show scared the bageebies out of me.

Other ways Philip and Gary would get under my skin, was when they would try to convince me that I was adopted. There were times we would be in the same room, maybe playing a game and they would start, "Cindi, you know you were adopted. Didn't Mother and Daddy tell you yet? They never wanted any more kids after Philip was born, but these gypsies came by and talked them into taking you. They felt sorry for you."

"THAT'S NOT TRUE!" I'd yell and try not to cry.

"Yes, it is. Think about it. We look just like Mom and Dad. You don't!"

At that point I'd go running to the kitchen screaming for Mother and through my wailing and crying I'd say, "Mom! Gary and Philip said I was adopted and a bunch of gypsies just left me at the house and y'all didn't want me but you felt sorry for me..." I went through the whole story.

"NO! That's not true - BOYS!" Mother would yell to their room, " LEAVE HER ALONE!

OK, so those mean brothers were just torturing me and it is obvious that I favor both of my parents and there is no way I could deny my Bradley/Strickland blood. In fact, many times Philip and I have been mistaken as being twins because we favor each other, so they say. No, I was not adopted.

As I've grown older, I've been intrigued with children who have been adopted. What a beautiful thought that a couple would take a child to raise as if he or she had been born to them. Some dear friends of mine in Tuscaloosa, Alabama traveled to Ethiopia and adopted a precious little boy. After two trips to Ethopia, appearing before a judge and going through an amazing ordeal, Anna and Tim Dreyfus were finally granted permission to give that little boy his name - Cooper Dreyfus. The legal documents proclaim that Cooper is their son and he has two brothers and a sister to help him grow in the Lord.

Another couple I know, Darryl and Carla Wood were granted a beautiful baby girl named Isabella. Other friends, Steve and Mary Jo Harris adopted their baby girl, Lexie, about 10 years ago. These children are blessed beyond words to have parents that love them and are raising them in the Lord and His church.

It took some time, but Mother finally convinced me that I was NOT adopted. "Honey, your brothers are just trying to aggravate you. You are NOT adopted!"

Or, was I? Yes, I know my Mother gave birth to me on September 23, 1961 at Saint Margaret's Hospital in Montgomery, Alabama. But, I'm still adopted. My heavenly Father adopted me and made me His own. As children of God, the same can be said of all of us. We're adopted. When I accepted Christ as my Savior and was baptized into His blood, I became a daughter of God. I was added to His family. Jesus is my older brother. Paul tells us in Galatians 4:4-7 that we are no longer slaves but sons. We receive the right to call God "Abba" which means "Daddy". We're made heirs and we receive the FULL rights of sons.

These adopted children that I've mentioned bare an amazing resemblance to their adopted parents. OK, maybe not Cooper since he's from Ethiopia and his parents are caucasian, but Lexie looks exactly like Mary Jo and Steve. Bella looks just like her Daddy, Daryl and even her big brother, Corey. In the same way, we're made in the image of our heavenly Father. We favor Him and people should know that we belong to Him because our lives should reflect Him.

Years ago, I remember a man by the name of Jack Exum who was a well known preacher and touched many lives with his stories and lessons on our Savior. I was in Junior High when he came to Montgomery and spoke at Landmark. He shared a story regarding the daughter he and his wife adopted many years ago. I don't recall the situation, but she had lived in their home for many years. As they sat in court, listening tothe judge give his decree, the little girl sat in Mr. Jack's lap. The judge continued with his "where untos" and "whatso evereths" and "from here into forward"...the little girl slipped from Mr. Jack's lap and ran to the judge. Just as the judge was about to finish, she grabbed the gavel, hit it on the desk and announced to the entire courtroom, "I'M 'DOPTED!"

The blood of Jesus makes the same declaration. My mean brothers were right - I **am** adopted...

...and for that, I say *"Thank you, Father."*

NOVEMBER - WEEK ONE

Are You Ladies Angels?   *Galatians 6:10*

If you've ever visited my home here in Huntsville or visited me when I lived in Chattanooga or Birmingham, you would quickly notice that I've never lived in a very elaborate home. Only when I lived with my parents have I ever been in a lovely, decorated environment. My Mother is a wonderful decorator and makes their house a beautiful showplace.

It's not that my home is not nice, but as a homemaker, I guess I'd fall far below Martha Stewart but several steps ahead of Fred Sanford. When it comes to decorating, I tend to side more with "sentiment" than I do with "elegance". For example, the pictures I have on my walls all have a story and a special meaning to me. Some of them are special gifts like the one over my sofa given to me by my parents.

One is a painting of the bridge in Destin, Florida, which is one of my favorite places in the world. I have a plaque given to me by my friend, Martha Kimbrough that reads: My three favorite places: the beach, the beach, the beach. In my living room is a print of a lighthouse painted by my good friend, Glenn Gray in Chattanooga.

I have an entire room in my house that I refer to as "The Alabama Room". My most prized pictures hang there including an aerial view of Bryant-Denny Stadium given to me by my best friend, Melisa. That one means the world to me because of all the fun times she and I have shared in that stadium.

Art can carry all kinds of meanings and bring all sorts of feelings to mind as you look at it. One of my all time favorite exhibits hangs over my kitchen sink. It was a gift over 20 years ago from a very dear friend in Birmingham. This classic work of art portrays seven dogs playing poker. Yes, dogs playing poker! I love that picture and anytime I move, it's one of the first items that I carry by hand into my new home. Occasionally my Mother will advise me, "Cindi, you need to get rid of some of this junk." Well, the picture of the dogs playing poker is not going anywhere!

"A Friend In Need"

In this picture, one dog is holding an Ace in his paw under the table and sneaking it to a fellow pup. The other dogs are either minding their own cards or shifting their eyes with suspicion to the guilty cheaters. The painting is called "A Friend In Need" and the expression on the benevolent hound shows true compassion.

One morning while filling a pitcher of water I looked at that picture and remembered the dear friend who gave it to me. Her name was Marsha Glenn and she was a true friend in every sense of the word. She was one of the first friends I made when I moved to Birmingham and began attending Homewood Church of Christ. We went to football games together, made beach trips together and enjoyed being involved in church activities. Anytime we had a "hankering" for something good to eat we would make a road trip to Tuscaloosa for ribs at Dreamland or go a little farther west to The Cotton Patch near Eutaw. Marsha always knew the best places to eat.

Marsha was constantly doing for others. One Sunday afternoon I remember her calling me on the phone and saying, "Come on, Reverend, we're going to UAB and make some hospital visits." She called me, "The Right Reverend Bradley" because that was about the time I began speaking at retreats and teaching Bible classes. She always said I was her favorite preacher.

At UAB Hospital, we visited a fellow member of our singles class who was recovering from an accident. After our visit with him, Marsha and I were making our way down the hall and passed a waiting room that was almost empty. I say almost, because there was one lady sitting there all by herself in tears. We stepped in, introduced ourselves and asked if we could help.

"My husband was taken to surgery and the doctor doesn't know if he can save him." We sat with that lady, held her hand, prayed with her, cried with her and just made sure she wasn't by herself during that upsetting time. Eventually, the doctor came out and told the wife her husband survived and will be fine. As we were leaving the lady tearfully expressed her gratitude to Marsha and me, hugged our necks and asked, "Are you ladies angels?" I almost laughed because, if she knew us a little better, she would have known we were far from it. Marsha quickly answered, "No Ma'am. We just like to go around bragging about Jesus."

I never forgot that answer and I remind myself of that statement quite often. As you may have noticed, I refer to Marsha in the past tense because she was taken from this life far too soon. In 1988 Marsha suffered a brain aneurysm and died. I still miss her and wish she was here but I would never want to take her away from the unbelievable joy she is experiencing in heaven.

From Marsha, I learned that we are most like Jesus when we are doing for others. The best way to reflect Jesus in our lives, is by serving others and being the "friend in need". The bragging is not on ourselves but on Him and His glory.

Day in and day out, you'll come across a friend in need. You'll come in contact with people who are hurting and facing difficult challenges. It's quite possible they're not going to come right out and tell you they're hurting or that they need help, but they're out there.

Take a moment to brag about Jesus. It might only take passing along a compliment to change someone's day. It might just be a word of encouragement or an offer to help them cope. It might be praying with them or letting them know you're praying for them.

Whatever that "ace under the table" is, hand it over.

Somewhere out in this big world, there's a friend in need.

NOVEMBER - WEEK TWO

Fill Your Cup With God   Colossians 3:4

It was a noisy Wednesday night at East Brainerd Church of Christ, but, anytime you're in a room full of 4 year olds you can guarantee it'll be noisy. My good friend, Julie Mathis had persuaded me to help her teach and it really didn't take much persuasion. It was a pleasure being in there and helping Julie. I spent most of the time just laughing at things they said and how fun they were.

As the children came in, we occupied their minds with puzzles, blocks and other activities until we started the lesson. Of course, we took the opportunity to sing some songs and try to focus their minds on spiritual things. Each child was so precious and so enthusiastic about being in Bible class. I was especially thrilled that Graham Hartness was in attendance. What a cute kid! I had enjoyed every minute of watching Graham grow from the first time I saw him in the baby window at East Ridge Hospital in October of 1999. He's the younger of two sons born to Dodd and Kelley Hartness. His big brother, Ralston was a little more laid back and low key and he too, was a precious little boy.

Julie and I managed to bring the children together in a circle for story time. She shared how we have many things that are important to us, but Jesus should be the absolute most important thing in our lives. Their little minds seemed to soak in each word Julie said and add their comments along the way.

Following the story, we had the children gather around the table as we prepared for an activity. Julie had stickers for each child. The instructions were, when we placed the sticker on their piece of paper, they were to tell us what number belonged beside it. The first was a sticker portraying a picture of Jesus. Julie held one of the stickers up and directed their thoughts: "Alright, boys and girls! Who is this?"

Each child answered quickly and loudly, "JESUS!" Julie then reminded them of how important Jesus is in our lives and what number should we place beside His picture - whether it should be one, two or three? It was unanimous: "NUMBER ONE!" Writing the number one doesn't require much assistance so each child made the mark beside their sticker.

The next sticker was various pictures of families; portraying Moms, Dads, kids, grandparents, etc...Julie asked again, "OK- here's a picture of a family. What number (after Jesus) would you put by this sticker?"

"TWO!" Again it was a unanimous choice. Each child, this time some needing assistance, wrote a two beside that sticker.

The choices for the third sticker varied. We allowed the children to choose a sticker that was their favorite thing to do. There were sports pictures, toys, Barbie dolls, and some blank ones where the children could draw their own choice. Julie then asked the children, "What do we put in our number three blank?"

Graham Hartness is 110% boy. Nothing girly about this kid. He jumped from his chair, held three fingers in the air and said loudly, "NUMBER THREE IS NASCAR!" His voice and the way he held his little fingers in the air was just like any avid Dale Earnhardt, Sr. fan.

Needless to say, I laughed so hard I hurt. I know it's one of those "you had to be there moments" but to see that little blonde headed fellow proudly hold up those three fingers and deeply profess his allegiance to "NASCAR" was hilarious. Being a NASCAR and Earnhardt fan myself, I couldn't disagree with him.

I couldn't wait to share this with Graham's parents and grandparents. They, too had a good laugh from that and to this day enjoy reminding Graham of the time he entertained Miss Cindi in Wednesday night class.

While that memory makes me smile, I also have thought several times about how we tend to categorize things in our lives. We put our lives in categories and we also place them in various compartments mentally. Priorities are extremely important but the problem comes when we do not allow our priorities to interact. In other words, we feel God and spiritual things are only for Sundays. Monday through Friday are strictly all about work. Saturday? Well, that's my hobby time or the day I get things done around the house. But, come Sunday, well...God is number one.

Gary Smalley explains it this way in his book *Love Is A Decision:* "we look for so many things to fill our lives or complete us, when in reality, it should be God that completes us or fills us. There are things or people that we are convinced we cannot function without. When these things or people do not meet our expectations, we are quickly disappointed. For some it's their spouse. Their life is not complete without a spouse or a spouse that must meet every expectation."

Some make their children their life blood and they would never be complete without children. There are people who make money their force in life and others make possessions or (this one hurts me) HOBBIES their completion in life. Smalley explains that spouses, children, money and possessions are gifts from God. GOD SHOULD BE OUR LIFE...not those gifts. Our cups are to be filled with God and the gifts are the overflow.

Making God our LIFE makes me realize that anything else is a gift from Him. He gives me the overflow of people, money, possessions and yes Graham - even NASCAR.

NOVEMBER - WEEK THREE

What's Your Hurry?   *Psalm 46:10*

It was one of those Sundays when we didn't have our children's worship known as "Celebration Station" at Mayfair. Just before the sermon, we sing a verse of "Jesus Loves Me" and the children are dismissed to the area where they have their own worship service and learn spiritual things on their own level. Many times, you'll hear sighs of relief from the parents and grandparents when we reach that part of the service. Once the kids leave, the adults can focus a little better. But, on this Sunday, the song was never sung. Children stayed where they were and every age remained in the auditorium.

"BE STILL!" The whisper came from the young mother as she watched her two year old squirm across the pew. Tara and Josh Minor have a beautiful baby girl named Katherine whose blue eyes stop traffic and her laugh is contagious. She's as pretty as her Mama and as sweet as her Daddy. With so much to capture her attention, sometimes it's difficult for her to stay still during an hour long worship service.

Just those words, "BE STILL!" coming from Tara brought a flashback to my mind. It's almost like Tara was speaking directly through my Mother's voice. Many times I felt those hands lift me by my shoulders and place my bottom on the pew with that stern whisper, "BE STILL!"

Dad loves to tell the story of his "try out" Sunday back in 1964 in Gadsden, Alabama with the Samson Avenue Church of Christ. He was a young up and coming preacher who was asked to interview for the pulpit minister's job and allow the congregation to hear him. It's the time when a preacher gives his best sermon and his wife and kids really need to be on their best behavior. Evidently, at two and a half years old, I missed the "be on your best behavior" memo.

Mom said I got a little fidgety and she had already given the order to, "BE STILL!" For some reason, I chose to ignore Mother's command and continued to squirm, wiggle and approach the line of being disruptive. To get my attention, Mother decided a good pinch on my chubby thigh would do the trick. She took a hunk of skin and gave it a good twist.

It got my attention alright! So much, that I decided to share it with the lady sitting next to me. I reached over and gave her a good pinch right on her arm. The bad news was, her husband was an elder in that church and one of the decision makers for their next minister. Dad got the job, but I'm pretty sure that was the last Sunday dear Sister Barfield sat with the Bradley family.

BE STILL!

Sometimes it's tough for a child and sometimes it's even tougher for a grown-up. Some of us take great pride in just how full our calendars can be. "I've got something to do every night this week!" It's almost as if there is a sense of accomplishment or prestige with the announcement to the world, "I'm just so busy."

The holidays bring a lot of hustle and bustle to our days. Shopping, parties, cooking, shopping, cleaning, decorating, shopping, another party and hey, I've got more shopping to do. We finish one family gathering only to jump in the car and head across town to another.

Our world has allowed the Thanksgiving holiday to become obsolete. Everything is so hectic that there is hardly enough time to BE STILL and be thankful. More and more retail stores are trying their best to get a jump on the "busiest shopping day of the year" by opening earlier and earlier each year. I remember not too long ago being amazed at stores opening at 6:00 am for that big day after Thanksgiving sale. Now half the day is gone by 6:00 am. Some major stores remain open on Thanksgiving Day and conduct business as usual. Oh, the drive of competition!

Maybe my Mother needs to give the rest of us a big pinch and slow us down. Maybe we all just need to take a deep breath, come to a stop and just BE STILL. We run in so many different directions, it's no wonder we don't have time to think...or maybe we just don't TAKE time to think. For some reason, someone or something has convinced us that where ever we are, whatever we're doing, there needs to be noise and something to stimulate our thinking. Children can no longer just ride in the car in silence or have a casual conversation with others. The DVD player must be going to entertain them and keep them occupied. Growing up for me, it was a life commandment that Sunday was a day of worship, then a day of rest. That's why they put golf games on TV on Sunday afternoons. That soft voice and slow pace of the game makes the perfect setting for a good nap. Now days that nap time has been replaced with trips to the office, showers and teas to attend, yard work and a ton of other activities.

David wrote in Psalm 46 "Be still and know that I am God." Let me challenge you to write that down in your calendar. Somewhere in your day, slow down, be quiet and BE STILL. Turn off the noise and turn up the quiet, because many times the silence brings rest.

In the silence, listen for His voice. Listen for whispers of His love. Just... be still.

Tara Minor with Katharine at nine months

I'm Starving   John 6:35

I remember back during my college years how much I looked forward to going home on the weekend. I was fortunate to be at Lipscomb and it was about an hour and 45 minute drive from the campus in Nashville to our house in Huntsville. The thought of being able to sleep in my own bed, wash a mountain of laundry and just relax for a day or so was something to long for all week.

My brother, Philip was a year ahead of me in school and on Thursdays we would decide if we were going home for the weekend or not. It was then I would make a call home and talk to my Mother. After some sweet talk and "buttering her up" ,I'd place my order for Sunday lunch. Roast beef, lumpy mashed potatoes, green beans, lime jello salad, homemade rolls and chocolate pie. It's still my favorite meal, as long as Mother is cooking it. I remember sitting in class and being so hungry for that Sunday lunch. I'd crave a hot roll oozing with butter. It was almost as if I could smell it all cooking right there in Elam Hall - only to wake up and realize it was an elusive dream.

What are you hungry for? Do you crave certain foods? Very few of us in this country go too long without eating, at least, not on purpose. Some do practice the sacrifice of fasting, but rarely do many of us miss a meal. Sadly, there are areas of this country (even right here in Huntsville, Alabama) where people are truly hungry, yes, even STARVING for something to eat. It's sad to catch some person digging through garbage dumpsters in hopes of finding a thrown out meal or even a sandwich. It boggles my mind to think that there are people right here in my own community that are actually hungry. Sadder still, to know that some are children.

HUNGER! Have you been there? Can you think of a time when you were so hungry you thought you would die before you got something to eat? I remember while traveling one time, I was waiting on a shuttle to the airport, and I went an entire day without food and when I did finally get the chance to eat - LOOK OUT!! It was eat or be eaten!

Have you ever seen someone hungry? I mean REALLY hungry. One cold rainy winter morning, I stopped at McDonald's on my way to work for a bowl of their hot oatmeal. I ordered my meal and made my way to a table., when a man walked over to me and said, *"Ma'am, if you have anything left over when you finish, please let me know. I'd be glad to finish it for you."*

My heart sank. Was he kidding? How could he not afford $2.50 for a bowl of oatmeal? He was ashamed as he asked me to throw him my crumbs. "Sir, take a seat over there and I'll bring you something to eat." I ordered him eggs, sausage, pancakes, oatmeal, coffee, orange juice and hash browns. His eyes were amazed as I placed the tray in front of him. He thanked me, said "God bless you ma'am" and bowed his head in prayer. I stayed long enough and watched him eat every bite. Who knows where his next meal was coming from, but for breakfast, he was getting more than he needed.

Was he a drunk? I don't know. Did he squander his money away on alcohol? I don't know - possibly. All I knew was, he was hungry and the way he tore through that breakfast told me he had not eaten in a long time.

HUNGER! What about spiritual HUNGER? Are you hungry spiritually? Do you crave the nutrition of spiritual words? Are you hungry to be around God's people? Just as I'm amazed by the abundance of hunger in this country, I'm also amazed that sometimes we go without spiritual nourishment. What amazes me even more is that we actually starve ourselves and cheat ourselves from a feast prepared by our heavenly Father.

When Americans are hungry, we fill ourselves with junk food. No nutritional value at all, empty calories. We often do the same thing spiritually. We're hungry for God but instead we fill our hearts and minds with junk, thinking it will sustain us.

Our Father not only has what you need, but He has more than enough to satisfy your craving. In fact, He is The Bread of Life. In John 6, Jesus is trying to explain to His apostles that they work so hard and worry so much over things that are perishable like food. In verse 27 He explains: "Don't waste your energy striving for perishable food like that. Work for food that sticks with you, food that nourishes your lasting life, food the Son of Man provides. He and what He does are guaranteed by God the Father to last."

I challenge anyone who has accepted the call and obligation to preach the Word on a regular basis to remember that people are HUNGRY. They so badly want to hear from you what the Lord has to say; they want to be challenged; they want to learn; they need direction; they need to be served the Bread of Life. It's so obvious in our churches, the ones that are growing and bringing people in have strong pulpits with preachers who share the word. It's not entertainment. It's not having their ears tickled. It's the churches that feed the hungry seekers with God's feast that are filling their buildings.

I also challenge the rest of us to go to the right source to satisfy our hunger. Jesus and Jesus alone has the right food for our spiritual stomachs. Don't settle for the drive-thru. He's got a special table waiting just for you - included is a feast unlike any other you'll find.

What amazes me is, not only does He provide the feast, He also paid the bill.

All we have to do is have a seat at the table.

DECEMBER - WEEK ONE

Rescue Me   *Matthew 11:28-30*

After getting all three of us out of college, raised and out on our own, Mom and Dad built a house in the rural area of Madison County, outside of Huntsville. They live on about nine acres just at the foot of Green Mountain in the little community of Owens Cross Roads, Alabama. The area where they built is known as "Possum Holler".

It didn't take long for them to become good friends with nature, more specifically, the animal kingdom. Mother made a pet out of a gray fox and fed her for about six months. That fox got a bologna sandwich every day and on many occasions, leftover casserole or meat from the house. We learned that foxes store food in their den to provide for their families and are also monogamous. You can't say that about many people. Sitting in their den, we love to watch the deer in the backyard. Dad has a salt lick set up, as well as a feeder that the deer can bump and corn falls out.

Stray cats have shown up knowing they'll get a good meal from Mom and there have been a few dogs make their way to their back yard. Maybe the animals talk among themselves and spread the word that the Bradleys in Possum Holler always have a place for them. Maybe that's why two obviously lost Golden Retrievers showed up one afternoon. It's very possible that someone was unable to care for the dogs and just dropped them off on the side of the road. They were domesticated but had no collars or any form of identification on them. They were wet, cold, hungry and extremely tired when Dad found them next to the garage.

If you're familiar with Golden Retrievers then you know they are very affectionate dogs and very much "people dogs". Experts will tell you, it is best for them to be house dogs and around people as much as possible. While it's true that they can be trained to be hunting dogs, for the most part they are to live inside. Knowing this, Mom and Dad had to find a suitable home for them. Not just anybody would qualify.

Dad brought the dogs in the garage, made a bed and began taking care of them. They even took them to the vet and it was confirmed they had definitely belonged to someone at one time and may have been mistreated. The female was painfully thin, weak and very lethargic. Her male pup was no more than a year old and very protective of his Mother. The vet gave them some needed shots, treated them for fleas and ticks and even gave the male some medication for the croup. The female was literally exhausted. The battle for survival had taken its toll on her and Mother was concerned she would even live through the night.

Proper meals were given, and a warm bed, but mostly love and affection for the dogs. Mom and Dad's garage is insulated and carpeted. Dad set up heaters and the dogs seemed to relax and were on the road to recovery. In a few days, they were running, playing and had that smile Golden Retrievers are known for. They were so cute.

Since at the time, Mother and Daddy already had a dog they knew they wouldn't be able to keep the dogs. They contacted an organization in town that rescues Golden Retrievers. They find homes for them and make sure the new owners are suitable for these type of animals. By early afternoon, the lady with the organization arrived at Mom and Dad's house, examined the dogs, thanked them for being such good humanitarians and loaded them in her truck.

Those dogs were not the same dogs when they left. They had been rescued. Just prior to the lady's arrival, the dogs rested comfortably in their warm beds with full bellies, cured croup and much needed rest. You could see relief and gratitude in their eyes.

Has the world thrown you into the cold? Maybe it's from poor choices or bad decisions, but are you worn out? Do you feel like you've been dumped on the highway? You can be rescued. There's a Savior that says, "Come to me. I'll feed you the bread of life. I'll quench your thirst with living water. I'll heal your diseases. I'll mend your broken heart." With Him, you'll always have a home.

Are you tired of running? You don't have to.

I beg you, PLEASE! Stop and turn to Him. He's the only Savior that pursues us.

We don't have to beg Him. We don't have to buy His love.

He just takes us as we are.

Take your shoes off and relax... *"welcome home"*.

Mom and Dad's beloved "child number four", Golden Retriever Bert

DECEMBER - WEEK TWO

Cry With Him — *1 Corinthians 15:55-58*

Although typical for December in Alabama, the weather was overcast, cold and rain was on the way. The skies depicted the feeling so many of us had in our hearts. It had been over 48 hours since we received word that Lisa Johnson had died, but the events of that terrible Thursday morning just wouldn't sink in. Very few people in Huntsville, Alabama didn't know Lisa Johnson; her sweet spirit and amazing Christian example. The city was filled with grief.

That Saturday morning Dad asked me to accompany him as he went to the house of David Johnson. David, or "Hoss" as he's been called for many years, met with Dad and Lee Milam, Mayfair's Worship Minister, to plan the funeral service for his wife, Lisa. Not really what he had in mind for weekend plans when the week began, but, following the events of Thursday morning, his whole world had been turned upside down.

Hoss sat on the couch with his huge loving arm wrapped around his 12-year old daughter, Madison. He spoke of songs and scriptures he thought Lisa would want and what type service should be conducted. Tyler, Hoss's 14-year old son, came in and sat on the other side of his Dad. It was obvious the children had not left their Dad's side very much the past two days.

The news of Lisa's death spread quickly, throughout the state of Alabama. Even Paul Finebaum, a sports radio announcer out of Birmingham, paid tribute to Lisa on his Friday afternoon show. Hoss is an easily recognized man in Alabama since he was an all SEC offensive lineman for The University of Alabama. He was one of the last recruits brought in by Coach Paul "Bear" Bryant in 1982, his red-shirt freshman season. Hoss spent four years protecting his quarterbacks, Walter Lewis and Mike Shula, with his strong arms. He spent the last 16 years protecting his wife and children with his heart.

Sitting in that living room, I was at such a loss. What do I do? What do I say? Hoss would speak and then a wave of grief would take over and the tears would flow from all of us. Lisa's precious parents, Jim and Dale Davis, sat with Hoss sharing his grief. Every now and then, we would laugh as one of us shared a special memory of Lisa. Lisa loved to laugh and you rarely saw her without a smile. She would want us to remember her that way, but the tears were hard to subside.

All of those comforting verses ran through my head. Knowing that one day we'll see Lisa again ran through my head. Thinking of Lisa obtaining that coveted reward that we all live for ran through my head. But, I didn't know how to put that into words. I didn't know how to say all of that to Hoss the right way. The truth of the matter is, even if I had said them, Hoss was so numb he would never remember them. They were just words.

I watched my Dad. This was not his first rodeo when it came to dealing with grief. In 50 plus years in the ministry, he had sat many times with someone who was hurting beyond words. But, to this day Dad would tell you that Lisa Johnson's death was one of the most difficult days of his ministry. Still, I knew he would know exactly what to say. He would say something so profound and even magical that would give Hoss, his children and Lisa's parents the comfort they so desperately needed. Dad had spent a lot of time with Hoss since arriving at the hospital that Thursday morning just before Lisa's death. As I watched Dad, his calmness, his confidence and his Christ-like demeanor was so evident.

Here it came. I searched my Daddy's face and quickly my mind went to John 11 when Jesus arrived in Bethany at the grave of Lazarus. Dad had said very little if anything at all. Just like Jesus, he grieved with them.

Our Lord approached those who were grieving, He let them speak and He let them ask their questions. He let them grieve and then He did the most powerful act of emotion ever recorded in the Bible. He cried. Did you catch that? Look in John 11:35. Yes, I know it's the shortest verse in the Bible, but, look at the context closely. He didn't just tear up or get a little weepy. HE CRIED! He cried so loud that others heard Him and commented, "Oh, how He loved Lazarus."

At the time when Jesus could have given His theological explanation of death and how we're all appointed to die one day, He didn't. He could have justifiably said that because it's in the Bible - Hebrews 9:27. He could have lovingly told Mary and Martha that we're not promised tomorrow and dying is all part of God's plan. But, He didn't. That's in the Bible, too - James 4:13. What did He do? HE CRIED!

My Daddy taught me something that Saturday morning. When people are grieving and feeling the worst pain they have ever felt in their entire lives, they don't want words. They need a Savior - and a friend who cries with them.

Thankfully, Hoss had both.

At a 2008 game with Hoss's daughter, Madison, and her best friend Lisa Copeland

Grace Is A Gift — John 3:16

It's that time of year again. Time for crowded shopping centers, long lines at the cash registers, cars circling the malls just looking for a place to park, sparkling lights in all the neighborhoods and lots and lots of food - everywhere you go. Yes, it's Christmas time. Every year I say the same thing; "Didn't we just put that stupid tree back in the attic a couple of weeks ago? Now it's time to drag it out again."

It comes around so quickly, or so it seems. It's always special, because we tend to make an extra effort to get together with people that we don't always see throughout the year. Office parties, church groups planning events, families traveling sometime during the season just to be together. Truth be known, I'd much rather a friend give me the gift of spending time together as opposed to spending tons of money on some item.

During the month of December, I always love to think back on Christmases as a child. I remember so many of them, but one particular year, I wanted to do something special for my Granddaddy Bradley. He loved Christmas. I mean really, LOVED Christmas. He wasn't one to go and buy a bunch of gifts but he definitely made sure anyone in need had plenty of food and some to spare. He delivered these items all over town to people he hardly knew. Knowing they needed help was all he needed to know about them.

Christmas 1974, I tried to save some money and buy something for Granddaddy. About a week before Christmas, I had $20 which I earned baby-sitting and all of it was going for that gift I picked out just for him. I had seen the commercials on TV and I just knew Granddaddy would love the Schick Hot Lather Machine. Granddaddy shaved every morning before going to work and I thought, how cool would it be to plug in that machine filled with his favorite shaving cream, let it heat up and then put it on his face! Total cost: $19.99.

I remember my Dad driving me to Service Merchandise on the Southern By-Pass in Montgomery so I could make my purchase. Dad had to help me out a little because I didn't have enough for the tax. At 13 years old, I was so proud and so excited about that one gift. It was all I could do to wait until Christmas Eve when we all gathered at my grandparent's house.

To know my Granddaddy was to know a quiet and humble person. He was a man of few words and got more joy from just watching everybody else and listening to the laughter. He'd get his fun in when he hid his cash gifts in the Christmas tree causing the recipients to hunt for them. But, when he received a gift, he didn't like opening them in front of everybody else. He never liked any attention drawn to himself so he would humbly place the gifts by his chair, opening them later in private.

The time finally came. We finished eating a delicious Christmas dinner prepared by Wo, my aunts and Mother then gathered in the living room, ready to open the presents. For the first time ever, I was more excited about watching someone else open a present, rather than receiving one myself. My Dad always played Santa and distributed the gifts one by one. "To Lisa from Wo and Granddaddy." My cousin opened her present. Dad would continue, "To Tommy..."

It seemed like forever and then finally Dad placed his hand on the wrapped gift. It was obvious it was from me by the way it was wrapped. I'll never win any awards for my wrapping ability. "To Granddaddy from Cindi." Dad handed him the gift as he reached for it and all of us expected him to lay it aside and nod a "thank you". Wo patted his arm and whispered, "Open it now and act excited." He smiled and began removing the paper. All watched as he looked at the package, figured out what it was and said, "Hey, this is great. Thanks!" It was an award winning act on his part but I was convinced he was thrilled to have his very own Schick Hot Lather Machine.

To me, that silly Schick Hot Lather Machine was the best gift EVER! I wanted him to have it and I just knew he would use it every day. For the first time, I saw how much fun it was to give.

Answer this question for me: What if? What if Granddaddy had opened that package, looked at me and said, "Cindi, I really don't need this gift. Why don't you take it back to the store and keep the money for yourself." A 13 year old girl could have done a lot with $20 in 1974. Movies were about $2.50 back then and a good burger and fries from McDonald's would run you less than a buck.

Had Granddaddy rejected my gift, I would have been crushed. It would have broken my heart. The hurt would be because I had invested so much into that one gift - not just $20, but the investment of my emotions. Seeing him smile and hearing that humble, "Thank you, Cindi" was total gratification.

Has anyone ever rejected your gift? Has anyone ever been so ungrateful for something you've bought or a deed you did just for them? Maybe it was more painful by what they didn't say or their lack of acknowledgment. It might not have been something that cost you any money. It might have been a kind gesture or an apology that you rendered and it went ignored or unaccepted. Perhaps it was just a compliment or encouraging word you gave and the recipient shunned you. How did you feel? Hurt? Embarrassed? Unappreciated? Unloved? All of the above?

The greatest gift of all was given over 2000 years ago. Our heavenly Father loved each one of us so much that He wanted to not only TELL us of His love, but SHOW us His love by giving. Giving absolutely the most perfect gift, the gift that no one else could ever top. The gift that cost more than anything we could fathom.

He gave His one and only Son, Jesus Christ. If I was the only one on this earth, God still would have given this perfect gift. Love was His only motivation for such a perfect gift.

Here's another question - what are you going to do with this gift? Do you accept it? Keep in mind you did absolutely nothing to deserve it or earn it. All you have to do is TAKE the gift. Will you do that? Will you unwrap it, smile, show it to others around you and spend every day of your life saying, "Thank you!" The best part of this gift are the blessings you receive from it every day. Every morning that you wake-up you have new blessings.

Rejecting a gift is painful...even to God.
Don't break His heart....accept His gift - and be thankful.

DECEMBER - WEEK FOUR

All I Want For Christmas — *Philippians 4:19*

It was a cold Christmas Eve and I was out begging for blood. I worked for a local blood donation center and blood supply was in high demand during the holiday season. If we could get some last minute donors, it would help us supply the local hospitals, as they too, prepared for the high demand. Standing outside in front of Wal-Mart was really not where I wanted to be, especially since the temperature had dropped and it was about to rain. Thankfully, there were others to chat with and pass the time.

The man standing next to me rang a bell luring attention to his Salvation Army kettle. In the course of conversation with him, I learned that he was a prominent businessman in town. He explained, that each year during the Christmas holidays, he wants to find a way to help people. Sometimes he helps serve the homeless in a local soup kitchen. Other times, he has helped distribute toys to sick children in the hospital. This year, he's a bell ringer.

It was during his sophomore year, as a student at the University of Alabama, that he took a job as a "mall Santa". He had me laughing until I hurt as he painted the picture of that experience. "My first day, I went to the mall office and the manager pointed at the Santa suit lying on the floor. It was a velour, red outfit with white trim." He went on to describe your basic outfit that you find on any Santa Claus. "No doubt, it had been 1960 since this suit had been dry cleaned. It wreaked of previous occupants and the scent from a spray can of Right Guard did no good whatsoever."

I asked him about the beard and he answered, "Oh, that was the worst. You know how sometimes a bad smell comes across your mind and it brings back a terrible memory? Well, that's what the smell of stale cigarettes and onion breath does to me. When I remember that smell, my mind immediately goes to that beard. Salem Lights and remnants of a greasy cheeseburger do not blend, but, I needed the money and it was steady work in 1980."

We laughed as he remembered the children. "Some of those kids are reasons why tigers eat their young." After going home, the ringing in his ears lasted as he tried to sleep. Moms and Dads forcing their children to sit on Santa's lap even when they're screaming in terror. Some would get quite impatient as they would wait their turn and if Santa didn't respond as they wanted, WHACK! A kick in the knee! "You came across some brats, huh?" I chuckled as I asked.

"Oh, you wouldn't believe how some of those kids would whine, complain, demand and not even come close to a 'thank you' as you sent them on their way. Some parents were worse than the kids. The bad ones were few but they certainly left an impression."

Then he got kind of serious on me. "There was one kid I'll never forget. You know, sometimes kids can hit you right in the heart and I'll never forget one in particular. It was December 23rd and the line to see Santa was so long. The chance for a lunch break or even a bathroom break was not feasible as more and more filed in. One little fellow standing in line caught my attention. His clothes looked old and maybe a little dirty. He was about seven, no older than eight. He stood there alone waiting patiently for his turn to sit with Saint Nick."

"He never seemed to complain or act impatient as he stood in line. He just quietly stood there, until finally, it was his turn. His brown hair was disheveled but his big brown eyes shined like a light on a Christmas tree. I helped him up on my left knee. I gave the typical, *'HO HO HO, WHAT'S YOUR NAME?'*

"My name is Michael, Santa, and I've wanted to talk to you for a long time." His enthusiasm was contagious and he could not stop smiling.

Santa knew he was on a time limit as others waited but he asked, "What would you like for Santa to bring you, Michael?"

"Santa," the boy humbly looked directly into his eyes, "I want a family."

A what?" Santa seemed confused.

"A family. I want a Mom and a Dad. I want to belong to somebody.

The little guy went on to explain how he had been placed in foster home after foster home and he had never known what it was like to be in a real family.

My friend said, "You know, Santa is supposed to be jolly and his belly is suppose to shake like a bowl full of jelly when he laughs. But, this Santa had tears in his eyes as he listened to this little innocent boy's humble request. No Power Rangers. No Transformers. No Lincoln Logs. ALL HE WANTED WAS A FAMILY."

"I didn't know what to say. I had just turned 20 years old and was certainly not experienced with this sort of thing. I just told him that there are some things that even Santa can't make or bring but God can. I asked him to trust in God and pray to Him every day. I tried to remind him, that no matter what, whether he's good or bad, God will always love him and he will always belong to God."

The boy wrapped his arms around Santa's neck, stepped down from his lap and Santa told him, "By the way, Michael. Santa loves you, too."

For the first time, Santa saw a smile come across the boy's face. He took his complimentary candy cane and walked toward the exit sign.

"THANK YOU, SANTA! THANK YOU!" "Cindi, I don't remember a single word another kid had to say the rest of the day. All I could think about was that little boy who just wanted a family - something I take for granted - something I thought everybody had but obviously, I was wrong. It's something that even Santa Claus can't fix. I'll never know if he got a family like he wanted. But, that little boy gave me a Christmas I've never forgotten and I think of him each year."

Love is what you hear in the room when you're finished opening all of the presents.

Dear Santa: All I want for Christmas is a National Championship!